Conversations With Top Real Estate Investors Vol. 4

With contributing Authors

Bob Snyder

Miguel & Connie Adames

Keith A. Cardinal

David & Gilda Couzins

Dr. Ram Mishra

Wojciech & Diana Przeczkowski

Shelley Sims

Landon Stokoe

Pat Walley

Charlyne White

Andy Wilkinson

Dominic Wood

Roxanne Young & Keith Miyamoto

Woody Woodward

D.U. Publishing
www.dupublishing.com

Warning—Disclaimer

The purpose of this book is to educate and inspire. This book is not intended to give advice or make promises or guarantees that anyone following the ideas, tips, suggestions, techniques or strategies will have the same results as the people listed throughout the stories contained herein. The author, publisher and distributor(s) shall have neither liability nor responsibility to anyone with respect to any loss or damage caused, or alleged to be caused, directly or indirectly by the information contained in this book.

ISBN: 978-0-9982340-7-6

Table of Contents

Introduction

Have you ever wanted to be sitting at the table when major real estate transactions were happening just to be able to glean insider information? If your answer was, "Yes" then this book is dedicated to you. You are going to be like a fly on the wall as top real estate investors are being interviewed and sharing their tips and strategies to being successful. These are honest and raw interviews with the intent to inspire you to follow your real estate dreams.

Bob Snyder

Renatus was founded and is led by 25-year entrepreneur, Mr. Bob Snyder. As CEO and President, Mr. Snyder is responsible for day-to-day company operations, affiliate marketing program expansion, course curriculum evaluation and renewal, practitioner-instructor recruiting, and month-over-month increased sales performance.

Mr. Snyder began his entrepreneurial journey over 25 years ago with the desire to leave a positive mark on the world. Establishing himself as a marketing leader, he gained first-hand knowledge of what drives marketing and team-building success. Mr. Snyder built and managed sales organizations with tens of thousands of individuals, achieved top status in multiple companies, and became a top income earner in the direct selling industry. He has freely shared his formula for success as he served on more than a dozen leadership counsels and advisory boards in the direct sales industry, received recognition in national publications as an expert in his field and has personally mentored over a dozen marketers to become seven-figure earners.

After years of building and growing marketing teams, Mr. Snyder's vision transitioned him into developing companies to expand the entrepreneurial spirit that has made this country the world's economic

1

leader. He has founded and co-founded dozens of companies that have collectively produced hundreds of millions of dollars in revenue. His real estate company completed over 2,500 real estate transactions while his former education company trained over 60,000 entrepreneurs on the subject of real estate investing and business ownership.

Contact Info:
www.MyRenatus.com

Shannon:
According to Forbes magazine, real estate is one of the top three ways that people become wealthy. As a real estate expert, why do you feel that this is the case?

Bob:
Because real estate is one of the three basic human needs: food, water, and shelter. There's always going to be a demand for real estate. Tech companies come and go, financial companies come and go, media companies come and go, but real estate is constant, and we are always going to have a need for it. Those individuals who position themselves with the right kind of properties are always going to be able to generate monthly cash flow.

Shannon:
Is that what inspired you to get into real estate: supply and demand?

Bob:
No. What inspired me to get into real estate was my wife. She dragged me kicking and screaming into real estate.

Here's the thing, I didn't understand it, and we always fear what we don't understand. I had been raised with the idea that a secure retirement required investments in the stock market. The problem was that I kept giving money to my broker and I continued to GET broker!

My wife was increasingly frustrated that we kept losing money on Wall Street, even from our conservative mutual fund investments. They weren't producing any kind of a sustainable return. By contrast, her mother and father invested in real estate while she was growing up. They made a habit of buying properties, paying them off, selling them, and buying others to build their portfolios. They developed cash flows that would take care of them in their retirement. Today, my father-in-law is eighty-eight years old and he and his wife live very comfortably from their paid-for real estate. The proof's in the pudding.

So, after losing a bunch of money on Wall Street my wife came to me and said, "Listen. We need to be in real estate. It's the way to build and secure our future and our kids' future. It's not Wall Street. It's not the stock market and it's not this other nonsense that you've been dealing with." Unfortunately, I was stubborn. I did not want to listen to her, but she was right and the last thing in the world I ever wanted was to tell her that she was right.

Shannon:
Now, looking back, you think, "Thank Goodness she was right."

Bob:
Yes, and think about what happened as a result of that, but it didn't happen overnight. She worked on me and worked on me, and I kept saying no. Then she finally came to me and she said, "Listen, Bob. I found this great little duplex. Its owner occupied on one side with a tenant on the other side, so the owner really fixed it up nice. The property is for sale by owner. We can get it a decent deal. It'll cash flow after we get a mortgage on it. You won't have to deal with it. I will manage it. I just need your support because if I don't do this I'm going to regret this rest of my life and you wouldn't want that, would you?" I mean, come on, what do you say to that?

Shannon:
You say, "You know, honey, I think we should get into real estate."

Bob:
I said, "You're absolutely right, but if this thing goes south I don't know if I'll be able to resist saying I told you so."

About a year later we were taking a look at the property's rents and depreciation schedule. All I could think was, "Holy smokes, we've got somebody living in our investment property who works all month long to make sure that we're the first one that gets paid. What an amazing business model." Then we get all these tax write offs, and the property was appreciating in value. This is phenomenal! It was one of those moments where I was like, "Wow, I'm glad I thought of it."

Shannon:

So when you were sitting in that real estate office, did she turn to you and say, "I told you so," or did she just say, "Bob, I am so glad you thought of this."

Bob:

You know, it's funny, Holly was really good about it. She just said, "You know what? You just needed to see it. You just needed to see it and do it," and she was right. All I could think to say was that we need to be doing a whole heck of a lot more of this, and that's what started our real estate investing career.

Back then we were so green, so naïve, we didn't understand real estate. We didn't understand wholesale buying opportunities. We did what 99.9 percent of the investors in this country do: go out, find a property, pay almost full price for it, put a tenant in the darn thing, and then you pray and hope that it's going to cash flow sometime in the next ten years. That's where our investing career started, but it gave me the bug and I had a desire to learn more, to grow in that business, to learn creative real estate strategies so that I could acquire properties for pennies on the dollar or buy them without any money out of pocket. I understood that with the right knowledge and drive to be a successful investor, I would never have to worry about money again.

Shannon:

Now, you've got all this knowledge and you've got years of experience, if someone wanted to get started in real estate, what would you recommend is the very first thing they do?

Bob:

The very first thing they need to do is get educated. That's just it. It's a business whereby if you know what you're doing you can make a whole lot of money and if you don't you can lose a whole lot of money. There is absolutely no ceiling on your income—the sky's the limits. You can become a millionaire, a billionaire, and I'm sure that down the road there will even be trillionaire real estate investors. The problem is, there's no floor either.

5

Shannon:

Yeah, I guess, if there's no ceiling...

Bob:

Yeah, if you don't know what you're doing, you can lose money. That's the biggest thing. You've got to get educated so that you have at least a common baseline of information, so you know how to fall in love with the deal and not the property. You need to know how to work the numbers and ensure that you are making a good, prudent business decision that's going to be profitable for you. The next thing is you've got to take action. I see too many individuals who fall into the category of what I call, educated derelicts. They're so versed on all sorts of different real estate strategies and different ideas, but they don't do anything with it. It's just fear that holds them back.

Shannon:

What do you do to get over that fear?

Bob:

Again, get educated. Education builds competency and when you feel competent about something you are more likely to take action. Action helps you to overcome fear, so the real formula for success is for a person to get educated and then to get busy. Education without action will not produce results.

For example, there are three types of students: the drop outs, the graduates, and the eternal. Those who keep learning and never start applying what they have learned continue to make up a larger and larger segment of our population. They are paralyzed by fear.

Let me give you an old acronym for fear

False
Evidence
Appearing
Real.

I believe that wealth is a mindset. Individuals start a conversation in their own mind that leads them to a certain belief, that belief either prevents them from moving forward or actually compels them to move forward. How they see risk plays an important role. Somewhere in their internal dialogue is a conversation about risk. When their focus shifts to all that can go wrong with an opportunity, they talk themselves out of moving forward with that opportunity.

That's why we build local communities of real estate investors all across the country. These local groups get together on a regular basis to talk about their real estate deals and what's going on in their business. When you've got somebody brand new who is fearful about fixing and flipping or building cash flow, it makes all the difference in the world to immerse them in an active community of investors. Surrounded by investors who are making offers, doing deals, and making money, a student gains confidence to make it happen for themselves.

At Renatus, we surround our students with examples of success so that they can get a realistic view of what it takes to succeed. In colleges and universities, students are stuck on the degree treadmill. They risk nothing and just keep going from class to class to class and degree to degree to degree. The lack of real world experience is the challenge with higher education.

Shannon:
Which becomes their new job.

Bob:
Yeah. It's not until they get into the real world that they start to experience anything. Believe me, I am a big proponent of education in whatever form that it can possibly come from. Unfortunately, higher education is letting more people down. They're getting degrees in fields of study that they will never make a living in and sometimes it enables them to just stay in that "safe" environment where they never take action which is why student loan debt continues to increase and student outcomes continue to decrease.

Shannon:
So, how do you change that?

Bob:

Specialized knowledge. It's unfortunate that the world of academia will never accept our type of educators because many of them don't have a college degree. Heck, some of them barely got their GED, but they are all successful, profitable investors. As for me, I got right into the world of business and by the time my friends were all graduating from college, I was making two to three times the money they were making.

Shannon:

How did you get educated? What did you do?

Bob:

You're going to love this story. I started my career in sales and marketing and then because of the frustration I dealt with working for someone else, I stepped into the wonderful world of owning and operating my own businesses. I had learned over the years how to build training platforms. I knew how to build sales teams. I knew how to create and build companies and I had a business partner who was also a seasoned entrepreneur. Together we were involved in a travel company but, after 9/11, nobody wanted to talk about travel; everybody was hunkered down and fearful of getting around the world. Our travel business really tanked. I did about everything I possibly could to get the wings back on the plane and make that thing fly again, but it just wasn't happening.

It was at that point that I had a conversation with my partner. I said, "Listen. Sometimes the best way to protect an opportunity is to create a new one." We owned real estate but we didn't understand wholesale buying or a lot about the real estate industry. I suggested we create an educational company centered on real estate investing. Then we hired the big gurus to come in and teach our people how to invest. The idea was that while our students learned, we would learn. What an idea, right?

That's where it all started. But the challenge was that the gurus we hired to teach students, students who paid good money to be in those classes, often refused to teach! They only wanted to whet the appetite of the listener so that they could up sell them to their own courses.

Shannon:
Oh, wow.

Bob:
So I talked to a friend of mine who had a PhD in Education. I told him we had a problem we needed to get beyond. Somehow we had to create a true learning environment instead of the ridiculous circus sales environment that our competitors used. He said he could help and we hired him.

He worked with us, and our staff, very closely for about a year. We brought in subject matter experts (SMEs) to help us take a good look at the real estate industry and construct our curriculum. We went out and organized focus groups from those who had paid money to gurus, both those who had and had not invested yet. All those focus groups assisted us in understanding what holds people back from investing.

We found there were four principle reasons for not investing: I don't have the time, I don't have the money/credit, I don't have the knowledge, or I'm just afraid. Those were the most common excuses. I view them as the excuses that cause failure.

Shannon:
I think we can say that for every aspect of our lives.

Bob:
Yes, we can. As soon as you start doing something, all of a sudden you say, "Hey, that wasn't so bad." I liken it to people who are W-2 employees. Most are fearful about whatever new thing they take on in life. For example, let's go back to the first day they started a new job or a new career. Were they a little intimidated? Were they a little nervous? If they're honest, they're always going to say yes. Fast forward six months. By then they have a pretty good handle on it. Most would say that they had gotten really good at their job and feel confident in it. The challenge is that they rarely ever feel like they are getting paid what they are worth?

We all go through that process. Fear is overcome through action.

We've got to get people in an environment that helps them to take one step after another. That's another thing I learned from Dr. Paul Ripicke. He taught us about the Instructional System design (ISD) methodology for curriculum building. It's what every major college and university in the country uses to build their curriculum paths and focus on student outcomes.

We thought, "well, if Harvard and Yale and Princeton are using this, we can use it too," so we went out and worked with individuals who were actual full-time investors in a specific strategy and we brought them on board. We worked with them to help us craft these classes, and then we taught them how to teach, and then we fired all the gurus. From that point forward, we had real-life investors standing up in front of our classrooms teaching our students. We forbid any of those instructors to ever sell anything in class because we knew that that would be a massive conflict of interest because the minute they started selling they would stop teaching.

Shannon:

Was there one type of person or personality that seemed to be most drawn to your classes or had the type of personality to be the most successful?

Bob:

It's not the personality, it's the circumstance. That's the one thing that all of our students shared; there was a heightened level of dissatisfaction with where they were. It didn't matter whether they were in a successful profession or they were just out of college struggling to make ends meet. They all had a level of dissatisfaction, whether it was enough time with their family, or a good enough future, or they were just sick and tired of working for a boss that didn't appreciate them. They all had a level of dissatisfaction. Again, wealth is a mindset. We just needed to give them hope.

Even for the staff who work here at Renatus, there's a huge shift in their mental framework. They may come in believing they need to contribute each month to their 401(k), but they end up learning how to do creative real estate investing to build their own wealth that they can control. It's pretty exciting to see that the staff members are also embracing the classes and getting out and doing their own deals.

Shannon:

It's kind of exciting because your employees could turn into full-time real estate investors and then you get to hire new employees and teach them, wouldn't you think?

Bob:

You know, there's always that thought in the back of your mind that, key people are going to start making so much money they're going to leave you. I encourage it, but over and over and over again I've got that same group of people who say, "You know what? This is what I want to do for the rest of my life," Renatus is a cause more than it is a job to them because they see the benefits that are showing up in other people's lives and that gives them a great deal of self-satisfaction.

Shannon:

Do you think students should find one real estate investing strategy and stick with that and become an expert, or do you think they should diversify?

Bob:

One of our favorite classes is understanding your investor ID because everybody's different. For example, some individuals have no problem going out there and buying property that they're going to put lower-income tenants into. They're just happy to get that check from the government every single month. Other individuals believe that if they wouldn't live in it, then they won't own it. We have different types of personalities and mindsets. They can all make money in real estate.

What we've got to do is figure out what their investor ID is: do they want quick turn real estate for lump sum cash returns or do they want to build cash flow over time with a nice, passive income from the property? I always tell people, once you figure out your investor ID, then you learn everything you possibly can about that strategy and you focus on that to become an expert.

But, you never stay stuck with just one strategy because markets shift and change. That's why we teach so many different strategies in Renatus. No matter what is happening with the market, no matter what is happening with the economy, if there's a shift or an adjustment in the real estate business and you haven't secured yourself with an understanding of different ways to get the same thing done, you're going to find yourself on the outside looking in and saying, "Well, gee, the economy's bad, so, the opportunity's gone." Not true, my educated students crushed it through the Great Recession. They made money hand over fist while everybody else was bellyaching and moaning that there wasn't an opportunity out there.

Shannon:

Do you have personally a favorite acquisition strategy? Which strategy just makes you the most excited?

Bob:

You know what, I love subject to, but this strategy died during the recession because equity went away and home owners owed more than the property was worth. When I started Renatus, over five years ago, I created a three-hour training series called "Fast Track to Financial Freedom." I showed individuals exactly what was going on in the marketplace, how they could capitalize on what was taking place at that time with real estate investing, and shared with them that we were about 5.2 million homes short of where we needed to be as a nation just to maintain the demand of housing for the increased population.

Many builders do not build in a recession; some went out of business and would need to ramp back up. This would not be an immediate fix. By the time you find raw land, go through all the entitlements, sometimes dealing with the city, and put a foundation in and start putting sticks up to frame the house, you're eighteen to twenty-four months out. It's not like this is just an immediate fix. You don't go, "Oh, there's a demand. I think I'll build a house here." It's going to take a while. I believed that once we got to the backside of the recession, there would be a great housing shortage and that housing shortage would create a massive adjustment in appreciation.

The good news is that the subject to real estate market has come back as prices have increased; we've seen a wild swing. Subject to is a great strategy because it's one of the best ways to acquire multiple properties and not be limited by banks and financial institutions. If you're dependent on conventional lending, you're going to be very, very limited in the amount of real estate you can do and the types of real estate transactions you can do. That's why I love a subject to–it's a great no money down strategy.

Shannon:
What about seller financing? If you're not relying on the banks, are seller financing and subject to the same thing?

Bob:
Well, yes and no. Some might refer to it as another form of seller financing because you are keeping the existing mortgage in place. Generally, seller financing is when a homeowner has a large equity position and they have the ability to create terms for the buyer to make the purchase.

Subject to is when you get the deed to the property, and you become the owner. It's yours. You own it subject to the existing mortgage, but the mortgage still stays in the name of the seller and they stay on the mortgage while you now own and control the home. Now, obviously, you've got to make sure that those payments are made, otherwise the lender will foreclose on the home and even though you're the new owner, they'll take it away from you just like they would have taken it away from the previous owner.

Shannon:
Is a subject to extremely risky as opposed to a standard seller finance, or are they about the same?

Bob:
Oh, no. When we discuss risk we have to think of who's at risk? The seller or the buyer? Individuals looking at selling their home using a subject to' are really in some serious financial stress and they know

that a foreclosure on their credit rating weighs heavier against them than bankruptcy.

Individuals that are stuck in that kind of a situation want to solve that problem before that property goes to auction and the foreclosure is complete. A smart investor will reinstate the loan and purchase the property subject to the existing mortgage. That way, a subject to helps the seller get back on track as far as reestablishing their credit, and it just takes a huge weight off of them. All the stress, all the burden, all the phone calls, all the challenges. It just takes it away so they can get a fresh start and go out and do their thing. The downside for the seller is what happens if the investor who bought the property doesn't make the mortgage payments.

Shannon:
That was my next question.

Bob:
Yep. What happens? Is there a risk? Well, absolutely there's a risk because then that seller could find themselves right back in foreclosure again. Of course, it's no different than the mess they were in to begin with so they're kind of back in the same position. But the bottom line is no investor that is really worth their salt is going to buy a property, put money into that property, and then lose that property because they aren't willing to make the payments. There's a level of assurance that everything's going to happen the way that it should happen.

Now as to the risk to the investor, it's pretty small. Worst case scenario you just walk away from the deal or give it back to the original seller and, if you haven't put any improvements into the property, you're not out anything. If you had put improvements in the property and for some reason you don't have the money to make those monthly mortgage payments, well, then shame on you, you're going to lose the money that you put into the property. Of course, an educated investor would just rent the dang thing out. Then you get a tenant making the mortgage payments for you. There's always a way if you know what you're doing.

Shannon:

That feeds back to all the different strategies. If I, as an investor, were to be in a tough spot and I had learned everything I could learn from you, it seems like I could go to my investment group and say, "Hey, who wants this property? I need help," and they would have the knowledge to help me out.

Bob:

Yep. Absolutely. You know it's just nice to have people that have been there, done that, to be able to pick their brain and lean on them from time to time. We've developed a really unique culture inside of Renatus. It's a culture of servant leadership, meaning that you never, ever ask anybody to do something you wouldn't be willing to do yourself.

If somebody in the community needs help and assistance then we have a pay it forward kind of mentality; but what I see from an awful lot of real estate groups out there, especially a lot of real estate groups, is that they're very motivated to try and maximize their relationships inside the club. There's so many investors in those things that are just looking to prey on brand new investors. They tell them they have a fantastic property that they could turn around and rehab and sell and make 50 grand, but they have to hand over a $10,000 assignment fee to get it.

Then, the brand new greenie goes and buys the property because some seasoned guy said it was going to be a great deal, and they find out that the price they bought it for was over-inflated, the supposed selling price was also over-inflated, and now they're going to lose money on the deal because they didn't know how to work the numbers for themselves. In our community, we apply a lot of emphasis on our leaders and on others in the company to make sure that we take care of community members because they're going to be with us for life.

With that continued emphasis, I outline for them how a deal should be done: Do not sell property to people in the community, unless we want to become a business partner with them, form an LLC with an operating agreement, and have exit strategies already spelled out; do not loan money to anybody in the community or borrow money from anybody in the community unless you become business partners, again with an operating agreement.

That helps to minimize risk. I hate organizations whereby brand new, especially green or naïve individuals get taken advantage of because they think that somebody is trustworthy. You must do your own due diligence because no one is going to care about your financial wellbeing as much as you.

Shannon:

You know, that is so unique to your organization and I love it. If more people just lived their life that way, not just in real estate but just lived their life that way, our world would be so incredibly different.

Bob:

We are all about student outcomes. When somebody buys an educational package from us, after the first year, if they're in good standing with the company, we convert them over to complimentary lifetime access. That means that they're going to have access to refreshed or improved and updated classes given to them for free, for life.

If we have new classes and new material that we roll out to the field, we just give it to our students, again without any additional charge. The complimentary lifetime access is a very, very coveted feature of the Renatus educational system.

Shannon:

You've done a lot of amazing things. You've built businesses, you've adapted, you're married, you have children, you have thousands of people that you mentor and that look up to you every day. What type of legacy to you want to make sure that you leave for them?

Bob:

Let me explain my motivation. The reason why I tick the way I tick, and believe me it's taken a lot of self-evaluation to figure it out, is that when I was a kid I had a father who was an alcoholic and a drug addict. His addictions created an enormous amount of financial stress in the home because we didn't know where our next meal was going to come from or what we would do when the power was turned off. I remember the bishop of our church was kind enough, when we lived behind him, to run an extension cord from his house over to our house so that we could run the refrigerator and watch Saturday morning cartoons after the power and the utilities had been turned off.

There was a lot of financial stress. I was a little kid and I didn't really understand it at that point, but as I started to grow it became more evident. The best thing that ever happened to Dad and the family was when he got caught for check fraud. That's what happens with addicts. They lie, they steal and they cheat, so that they can feed their addiction. Best thing that ever happened to him was he went away to jail for two years. Prison was a forced rehab for him.

When he was sober my Dad was a pretty brilliant guy. He graduated top of his class from University of Pennsylvania, and he went on to get his law degree from there. He was an assistant district attorney in San Francisco and had his own private practice up in Seattle. I mean, he was a smart guy. It was just addiction had taken a toll.

The other thing that meant a lot to me was my church, my faith. I served a two-year mission for my church. I loved every minute of it, being able to teach people how to apply gospel principles to bring them a lot of joy and happiness was rewarding. When you take that kind of philosophy and those correct principles and you put them into business with an investment like real estate, you can teach people a career path that will give them security, stability, financial freedom, and independence. You allow them to then give back to the community and to the world, and you can leave your kids and grandkids a lasting legacy from the inheritance they'll receive when you finally finish your time on this planet.

For me, all of that really has kind of led me to where I'm at today. My greatest satisfaction comes from seeing our students actually do what we teach them how to do and succeed. It comes from seeing them be good stewards of the money that they make. That's another thing, I'm not one of these flashy guys. I've got a nice house and I've got some nice cars, but I'm not driving around in a million-dollar Lamborghini.

There's not a lot of the flash and the bling and the nonsense with me because I don't want to set a bad example for my team. I would rather talk to them about cash flow. I would rather talk about assets. I would rather talk about balance sheets and profit and loss statements and how they can improve their lives and what they're doing to improve the lives of others. If I can make an impact on the community that really transforms their way of thinking so that they act and behave in that manner, we'll change the world.

What brings me the greatest amount of happiness is that I love seeing the positive changes in people's lives. In my first real estate company I dealt with a business partner who lost his focus. His ego got out of hand and he forgot about the people. It was all about his ego and his own self-aggrandizement. His world got so big that he just found himself working harder and harder to feed the monster of his creation. He had an enormous house and expensive cars and private servants and nannies and security details. He even had a jet.

I was just so disappointed with him; he set a bad example for the team. A lot of people in the community wanted to be like him. They started to make really bad financial decisions and leverage themselves into cars and houses and things that weren't producing income for them. He ended up filing for bankruptcy and had to liquidate millions in personal debt.

But life was always good for me because I've always lived well below my means. There's a massive lesson in that. Be a good steward of what you've got, live below your means, and you can still enjoy life, and I do. I enjoy life, and I don't have financial stress, and if everything but my real estate was taken away from me today I would still make a really nice income and never have to worry about money the rest of my life. I want people to have what I have. That's why I do what I do.

Miguel & Connie Adames

Miguel Adames is a real estate investor and CEO of AJMAX REI. He is passionate about real estate and its possibilities. Miguel is no stranger to hard work, having spent 20+ years in manufacturing and as a shipping foreman in Chicago, where he was born and raised. He understands what it means to have the security of your own home. He co-founded Lighthouse Business Development Group and AJMAX REI with his wife. He is passionate about real estate investing and its possibilities. Miguel provides real estate workshops services that help first-time homeowners, mortgage acceleration, real estate investing, and business networking.

Connie Rivera Adames is an Illinois real estate broker with EXIT Strategy Realty. She is proud to help buyers, sellers, and investors purchase and sell properties across Chicagoland and the state of Illinois. She specializes in helping first time home buyers, new investors, and single parents purchase their first home. She is fluent in both Spanish and English. Born and raised in Chicago, she has a passion for the heartbeat of the big city but has also lived in Puerto Rico and the Virgin Islands. She has over 20 years of experience in sales and 15 years of Executive Administrative support. Connie is also no stranger to entrepreneurship as she started her first business when she was 18 selling beauty products. She also owned a scooter shop in the Virgin Islands, as well as a cosmetics boutique. She is currently the President of AJMAX REI, Inc. and co-founder of the Light House Business Development Group in Waukegan, IL.

Connie and Miguel have been married since 2012. They have five beautiful children: Alycia, Joseph, Matthew, Albert, and Xavier, ranging in age from 12-20 years old. Together they created the AJMAX Team, and they all work in the family real estate investing team. They all play a role from advertising to social media and from administrative tasks to repairs.

Connie and Miguel offer a broad range of programs and public speaking services from financial literacy education to mortgage reduction strategies to first-time home buyer seminars.

Passionate about real estate investing and its possibilities, they provide networking opportunities for real estate investors that help both the rookies and the seasoned investors to achieve their goals through the Lighthouse Business Development Group out of Waukegan, Illinois.

Contact Info:

Connie and Miguel Adames can be reached at: 847-693-6200
or by email info@lighthousebdg.com
Website: ConnieTheRealEstateAgent.com
Twitter: @LighthouseBDG

Shannon:
Did you both always know that you wanted to be in real estate investing?

Miguel:
I never imagined myself as a real estate investor. I couldn't even imagine myself as a homeowner until a few years ago when I had the opportunity to dive in and look at all the possibilities that are available through real estate investing. I knew I wanted to make a difference in my community creatively or artistically as an artist. Through real estate investing, I have the opportunity to create true financial freedom so that I can make a difference and share my passion for art.

Shannon:
What about you, Connie?

Connie:
I have been always curious on real estate investing. I understood that it provided freedom. In the 90s, I attended those weekend real estate seminars to receive the free books. I also bought all of Robert Kiyosaki's books on real estate investing. I was inspired to get started in real estate in 2008 by my three-year-old son. At that time, I was recently divorced, a single mother, and living in a small two-bedroom basement apartment.

My son was a huge fan of Thomas the Train, and he asked me if I would paint his room Thomas the Train Blue. I explained to him that I couldn't, because we didn't own it. I told him that we only borrowed the apartment every month and paid the owners to use their space. Then, my son said something that was as simple and easy as only a three-year-old could comprehend. He said, "Mommy why don't we buy it and paint my room?" Two years later, we bought a two flat in the Westside of Chicago. It was that simple. What's the problem and the problem was solved.

Shannon:
You know, Connie, I have to ask. Does your son have a blue room now, or did he get over that?

Connie:

After two years of waiting, he got over painting his room that dark blue.

Shannon:

I'm sure you would have done that, though, right?

Connie:

Sure, I would have.

Shannon:

Miguel, what inspired you to get started in real estate?

Miguel:

The thing that got me inspired in real estate is the creativity of making something out of nothing. I always like creating, fixing, and building things. It was that aspect of real estate inspired me. When I was 18 years old, I wanted my own apartment but couldn't afford it, because I was sponsoring myself through college. My mother had a large unfinished basement, and she told me if I wanted it then I had to build it out. So, I did. I built a two-bedroom apartment, with new floors, a kitchen, a bathroom, shower, electrical, and even heating equipment. Mind you, I didn't have YouTube at that time. I bought and borrowed books. My uncle taught me how to do some of the stuff, but for the most part; I did it. It took a long time, but it was worth it.

Shannon:

Connie, tell me. What is one of the top real estate strategies that you have learned?

Connie:

One of the real estate strategies that I learned was the benefits of rentals. One thing that I learned through being a real estate student was to take the time and find out what I like to do and don't like to do, and do more of the things that I love. Being a landlord, gives me the opportunity to not only create cash flow, but also gives me the opportunity to give back to the community that I am investing in by being a responsible real estate investor and landlord. I got the chance to provide beautiful, safe, and economical housing that will create amazing family memories. Creating cash flow and passive income is awesome; building safe housing is world changing.

Shannon:

Miguel, what's one of the top real estate strategies you have learned?

Miguel:

When I first found the education, I wanted to find them, fix them, and flip them. As I continued to learn more about myself as an investor, I found that I enjoyed the opportunity that was provided with buying properties, renting them out, and taking care of them. That's sexy to me, so is passive income, I love that part; I plan to create a bunch of those.

Shannon:

Well, you know if you're talking about building; what does somebody need to know if they want to get involved in multi-family dwellings?

Miguel:

Know your numbers. The numbers must make sense to you and your investors. All the numbers, even those little numbers like taxes and water or utility bills. Something small could turn out very big. You should always cover your bases, and ask a lot of questions.

Shannon:

How has your education in real estate changed the way you invest?

Miguel:

That's a good question. Let's see. You know what? I didn't want to invest in property but because I know what I can do, now I'm saying that the sky's the limit. Every time I drive around, I look around, and I see a lawn that is not very kept, I think, "Oh, this look like they haven't cut the grass for a while. I wonder if they're still there, I wonder if they are interested in selling their property." I see opportunities in everything, and because I have education, now it makes me bolder, to want to be more, to dabble more into investing and taking on the opportunity in buying apartments, and more buildings—whatever I see, it's available to me.

Shannon:
If you're starting with little money or poor credit, are there any strategies to help you get started in real estate?

Connie:
Retirement funds. So many people are getting little returns, no returns, and even losing money in their retirement programs, and with several retirement savings, real estate is the product you can invest in and get high returns. Double digit returns on potentially stagnant funds—now that to me is sexy.

Shannon:
In your business, how do you help other people become sexy? I'm just kidding. In your business, how do you help other people learn more about real estate?

Connie:
I help other people learn more about real estate through social media, through word of mouth. I'm also a real estate broker with a local brokerage, so it is very important for me to teach buyers, sellers, and investors the importance of knowing their numbers and being responsible as an investor, as well.

Shannon:
Miguel, what do you think is the number one mistake an individual makes when buying their first investment property?

Miguel:
Not knowing the potential red flags of the property, not knowing the numbers; making sure the numbers set well with what you are trying to achieve, and that the figures are correct. You can make a simple mistake, and your fix and flip could turn out to be a flop and flop.

You might come into more repairs that you weren't expecting, but if you don't plan that exit strategy, and then the next exit strategy, that could hurt you in the long run.

Shannon:

You guys have both said, knowing the numbers, knowing the numbers. What are the numbers?

Miguel:

The numbers would be the cost of repairs, the closing costs, and the time line you want to be in and out of the project if you are doing a fix and flip. You would want to have a buyer before you even get into a property, so you should have a buyer's list. So, you already have pretty much the property sold before you even start the repairs. You don't want to be sitting on a property for a certain amount of time which you didn't plan for, depending on how you acquired the funds, and if there is interest involved that can be very expensive.

Shannon:

Connie, when you're doing a fix and flip, what do you look out for?

Connie:

When I'm doing a fix and flip, I look out for a couple of things. For me, the best money maker for a fix and flip, in my opinion, is the area and the school district. Especially living in the Chicagoland area, as families grow, they're looking for better schools. So, I like doing fix and flips in the better school districts. It's like looking for that diamond in the coal mines and then being able to make it beautiful. That's what I look for in a fix and flip. A great school district, enough work, but not enough work where you lose a lot of money, but enough work to make sure that you double up on your profit, at the minimum.

Shannon:

Is double your standard?

Connie:

Double on what I put in?

Shannon:

Yes.

Connie:

That would be super amazing. Depending on how I structure the deal would depend on what my expected returns would be. Sometimes, I have a dollar amount that would make the deal worth my time, sometimes it's a percentage number.

Shannon:

Miguel, what's cash flow, and why should it be an important focus of your business?

Miguel:

When you're buying a property, and it's a rental, you need cash flow. It must be the right amount to fit the building, and the needs of what the property's going to take. Being able to generate money to build for more other properties is also great, so cash flow is very important when it comes to rentals.

Shannon:

Miguel, you touched on how you want to make sure it covers everything, so you've got cash that comes in and you want to make sure it covers everything.

Miguel:

You want to make sure, especially if you're anticipating a certain amount of cash flow, that you include some of the simplest things, including the water bill, any maintenance, the taxes, all these different things that could impede how your cash flow would go, especially on multi-units. Cash flow is like the money, the total money, liquid money, that's available to you. You want to make sure that it is all coming to you.

Shannon:

You don't want to get dehydrated.

Connie:

You want to make sure that you get your money. That's pretty much it... and you want to make sure that you know how much you're spending, and you want to make sure that you know your numbers. What's the water bill like? And if you don't know what the water bill's like, you can go to the village and find out what they paid in the last 12 months, or what the average is in the neighborhood, or the average for that property is, so that you don't get crushed afterwards.

Shannon:

In your buying homes, do you manage them yourself or do you have a property manager?

Connie:

The properties I have purchased I have managed.

Shannon:

At what point do you think you will hire a property manager?

Connie:

I have not set a particular number of doors that would then encourage me to have a property manager. I understand the value, and I completely understand the benefit of it, but I have not set a number as of yet. I can say that I am playing that by ear.

Shannon:

So currently you invest in the state.

Connie:

Yes.

Shannon:

What other states are you interested in investing in?

Miguel:

We have considered Puerto Rico. Florida is another state we are looking into. Currently, we want to stay local because we want to get our hands in it to feel it, and then once we get a good understanding of it, then we are going to spread out.

Shannon:

When you began your real estate investing career, how important was it for you to establish a team to help you be successful?

Miguel:

I think at the beginning, we weren't even thinking about "team." We thought we had to do it all ourselves. As we continued to grow as investors, we realized that it is important to build a team, within our Investor community as well as our transaction team, and our team within the real estate network

Shannon:

How do mentors in your real estate investing community help you navigate potential pitfalls?

Miguel:

Oh, they've been great. The education is great and the mentors are patient. We've had to talk to them at two or three o'clock in the morning—you realize, "You know, I need to call this person," and you realize it's one o'clock in the morning. You're like, "Oh, I'm so sorry I called you so late," and they're like, "Hey, I was up, too. Go ahead; What's your question?" So, it's been great. They've been so welcoming and so inviting and it' been great.

Shannon:

Connie, do you have anything you would like to share about how a mentor has helped you navigate a potential pitfall?

Connie:

I think the most beautiful thing about mentors, especially in the real estate community that I belong to, is that they are filled with such a wealth of experience and education, and with such a willingness to assist others in the community. I appreciate even their openness to share their failures, that's the importance of having a mentor, and then you want to make sure that you connect with someone that's going to tell you if you're making a mistake or not. And that's what I appreciate about mentors. They're there for you. They're not afraid to tell you whether you're doing wrong or right and they're not afraid to tell you if they make a mistake.

Shannon:
What advice would you give to someone who is allowing fear to hold them back from starting their real estate investment career?

Miguel:
Get educated. Gaining knowledge reduces the fear. If you are knowledgeable and become the expert on what you're doing, you won't have any fear because you'll know what you're doing, there's nothing to worry about. You'll have all aspects covered, and you'll know what to expect and be prepared, and then on top of that, the mentor is there to help you, guide you.

Shannon:
How does learning multiple investing strategies protect and accelerate your investing success?

Miguel:
By learning multiple strategies you will have the knowledge to engineer different transactions that will create the best opportunity for you to protect your investment. You will have the opportunity to combine two or more strategies that will help you achieve your goal.

Shannon:
Connie, do you have anything you'd like to add to that?

Connie:
I think it's imperative to learn multiple investing strategies. It might start

out as a buy and hold, and then you realize you don't want to keep it and then it will end up a fix and flip. Or it might start out as a cash purchase, and then you see another deal that you might want to do, so you choose to owner-financed and then buy and hold it, and then end up fixing and flipping it. So, it's important to know all the different strategies and how they work and how they can work together so that you can provide the best solution for whatever problem that you come up with.

Shannon:
Is real estate investing success dependent on a strong economy?

Connie:
I don't believe so. It's dependent on a high education. There are strategies for everything. It's not so much about the economy. It's more so about what you can do with the knowledge that you have acquired.

Shannon:
What do you think, Miguel?

Miguel:
I agree with that. It's not about the economy because people always need housing; people always need food. That's something people are going to need as long as we're humans; we're going to need these things. There's always going to be a need, and we could help solve someone's problem with housing and make a little money, why not?

Shannon:
What good strategy is used to acquire a property during a strong economy?

Miguel:
Where a healthy economy, people will be saving more and be more willing to invest, so you'll get a lot more people using 401k and other savings to purchase properties.

Shannon:
What is a short sale?

Connie:

A short sale is a long process.

Shannon:

How long does it usually take from beginning to end?

Connie:

Oh my goodness. Short sales are so useful. A short sale is generally a sale where the owner falls off a little bit on their mortgage to the point where the bank is threatening and saying they're going to take away their house, and say all these really nasty things to them. Through the short sale, there is an opportunity for the homeowner to come out really well where they don't get the full value of their house, but they can sell their home at a reduced rate and still keep the honor of whatever credit that they can still hold onto without having a bankruptcy on their record. Because, those stay on there for a long time. Short sales are designed in that they can last anywhere from 90 days to a year, maybe even longer, depending on different things, but they're not short at all, and it's a lot of paperwork. It's all well worth it. As real estate investors, there's a lot of opportunities and deals that come out of those short sales, but besides that, we also have the chance to help a lot of different people that don't know what else to do to try to save their credit.

Shannon:

How do you help people save their credit by making a short sale?

Connie:

With a short sale, you have the opportunity to buy their homes, as opposed to having the bank take it away from them. So, when the bank forecloses on them and takes the house away from them, that stays on their record for quite some time and usually when that happens, you have to file bankruptcy to try to clear your name up with some things and try to get a fresh restart and that's just so hard for so many different families. With the short sale, you have an opportunity to save them from getting their home repossessed from the bank, and that's a life changer for some people.

Shannon:
Why do you think people fail at real estate?

Miguel:
They're not prepared. They didn't do the research, or they miscalculated on the numbers or misjudged. There are quite a bit of way where people could make a mistake or someone could fail. Being prepared, though, and knowing what you could have afterward, you'll build up for that. Nobody ever makes every single purchase or buy 100 percent correctly. People make mistakes. Some of the best mentors will tell you that. They made quite a bit of mistakes but by being prepared and being educated you'll survive that.

Shannon:
Connie, why do you say people fail and on the flip side, why do you think people succeed?

Connie:
Failure and success are how you show up in life. If trying something that didn't give you the full results that you wanted and you learn something in the process, you were successful in learning what not to do that gave you the results you didn't want. If you learn something in the process, did you fail? No, not at all. You'll do better the next time. It's the same thing with success. It depends on what you measure it as. You could define your success based on how much money you made or how many real estate deals you have completed, but you could lose the respect of your friends and family in the process. You may have decided to lie, or got greedy and decided not to pay people you solicited to assist you in your projects, but you completed millions of dollars in deals, are you successful? There are several adjectives that would describe someone like that in my opinion, and successful is not one of them. That person may be rich in coins, but he is poor and maybe even bankrupt when in the currency of relationships. Every day we have choices. Every day we learn. It's about how much more did I learn today, so I don't make that same mistake tomorrow. For me, it's about being complete in my

successes and learning from my short comings so that I can do better and be better. I am in no way where I aspire to be as a real estate investor, and I have gone past where I used to be as an investor, and I continue to grow and learn.

Shannon:

That's refreshing to hear. It's always interesting to see how different people and different personalities define success and failure, so I always enjoy these interviews when people talk about, "Well, what's your definition of success?" So, thank you, Connie.

Connie:

You're welcome, Shannon.

Shannon:

Connie, I'm going to have you answer it first and then Miguel—how has real estate changed your life?

Connie:

It took me two years to purchase my first investment property, because I had to rebuild my credit from a divorce. When that real estate transaction finally went through, and I received the keys, and I not only had my first home but an investment property, I was like WOW! What can't I do! I was a single mom. I was living in a little basement apartment; I could hardly afford childcare sometimes. I was told that I chose the hard road because I decided to be a single mother instead of being in a marriage where my husband at the time was unfaithful. I was told that I couldn't buy a home because of how little I made. I was told a lot of things. When that deal went through, and it included the income that was coming through with the current tenant with the property that I purchased, that was a game changer for me emotionally and intellectually. When I acquired the first one, that was a huge game changer, and it has been like flying on roller blades ever since then, just going for it.

Real estate investing not only changed my life; it changed the life of my family as well. The real estate education and the community that I am currently a member of has changed our lives because not only are we learning about real estate, we're learning about basic life skills and financial education. This changed how we live our life, our children's life, and their children's life. It has changed how we deal with money, how we build relationships, and it has opened our eyes even more to how we deal with all of our different currencies that we exchange with other people. So, this education has been a game changer and a life saver for our family.

Shannon:

Thank you, Connie. Miguel, what would you like to add to that?

Miguel:

I would like to add that I have to agree with my wife. When I learned about real estate, and I was sharing what I learned about with every-body, I would be so excited: "Hey, I learned this, I learned that," and then I would have people come to me, saying "You know, I want to buy property and I got loan," or "I can't find an area, and I don't know what to do. I don't know how to fix my credit, and I just need advice."

Being able to guide people in the right direction, have them talk to the right people, get them the information they need to make the right decisions for themselves and their family, it was a simple fact that I helped somebody and that's what I wanted to do. That's the type of person I am. I always wanted to help people, and I didn't know a good way to do that, and I now realize that you could do that with real estate.

You could be the help that a family needs. You could change their life and their children's lives. That is such a blessing in itself. You know you're doing something right when it makes you feel like that. I can't say how much more I wish more people would see real estate that way.

Shannon:

Now if someone wanted to get started in real estate and they came to you for advice, what would you recommend they do first?

Connie:

The very first thing that I would truly suggest is getting an education. There is no better prevention of fear then preparation, and the first thing I would tell them is to get educated. I would recommend the Real Estate Education Program that I'm participating in: #1 Get the "Know."

Shannon:

Miguel, what would you recommend they do first?

Miguel:

That's the perfect answer—education. With the education, with the community we're also involved with, or for the networking that we're involved with, that knowledge you can't find anywhere else. You can't pay for that somewhere else. That knowledge will conquer all your fears, all your worries. If you put a little bit of work into it, you could be the expert, and you won't have to worry about fears. You just do it.

Shannon:

In your interview, your answers have been so complementary. Usually, with couples, you get very distinct personalities where you can see,' okay, this person is this and this person is that.' You two seem to be very similar, yet different. I can tell you complement each other well, but I thought, I'm going to ask them this. You might be the first couple who has never disagreed on whether or to buy a property because your answers have been so similar. Well, in the long run, you both win, because you're married and you love each other.

Connie:

And we all win.

Miguel:

All she got to do is give me that face, and I'm like, "Okay, you win."

Shannon:

What is the legacy that you would like to leave behind?

Connie:

The legacy that I would like to leave an abundance for my children and my children's children. I want my family to be abundant in love, prosperous in relationships, and rich in financial wisdom. The legacy that I want to create for my children is that they can have it all. There is no limitation to what they can have except the limitations that they create in their minds. The legacy that I want to leave in this world is that it's possible. Whatever you think, whatever you dream, those are your dreams. Both were given to you as a gift, and you can have that, too.

I strongly believe that God put me on this earth to help parents teach their children financial literacy so that their children can teach their children financial literacy.

Shannon:

Thank you. Miguel, what type of legacy do you want to leave?

Miguel:

I grew up in a poor environment, and I was taught by my mom to pray for what you want, try to get what you can, and what you didn't have wasn't meant to be. I had to learn to change that philosophy because that was blocking myself off to the possibility of abundance, and that's what I have being teaching my children. I want to teach my children through real estate investing, that, there is an abundance of wealth and relationships for them. I realized that the world is my oyster and I could have anything I want if I worked hard for it, so I put in the work and put everything on the line and go for it, and you can have anything you want. They need to understand they are influential people on this earth, and not for themselves, because I don't believe in 'for me,' I believe in for others. I believe in for everyone. If they win, we all win, and that's how I want my legacy to be, that I was that person who stood for everyone and brought everyone with me.

Keith A. Cardinal

Originally from New Jersey, Keith and his wife Laura of 38 years moved to Arizona in 1994 where they raised their two sons now both successful in their own right. A graduate of Michigan State University, where he and his wife met, he studied Package Engineering and worked for various multi-national corporations designing and developing award-winning packaging.

Keith has successfully built teams and managed projects for major enterprise companies and small start-up concerns. He was a Global Director for a major FMCG prior to moving into consulting and real estate investment. Solving pain points for major enterprise organizations is his forte as owner of his current consulting company and is essential in solving real estate challenges. He helps mentor new entrepreneurs on key foundational financial and business principles, enabling them to present to investors. He is a sought-after mentor for start-up incubator clients and new entrepreneurs.

His life-long entrepreneurial spirit is evidenced in his ventures including owning his own construction company in New Jersey where he designed and built high end modular spec homes, acting as the General Contractor while working for a major health care company. After relocating, he formed a design and fabrication company building equipment for the global chemical packaging industry.

Keith is now an active real estate Investor, managing or funding multiple rehab projects. He is also active in private money lending and teaching others how to obtain financial literacy and free up retirement assets to invest in real estate. Long term, his focus is on rental real estate and building a passive income stream. He is associated with a nationwide community of real estate investors working on joint ventures and helping to inspire other new investors in the value of following proven success systems. His goal is to continue to build on this strategy as well as renovation projects in order to establish a portfolio of long term rental properties.

Keith has always had a strong desire to give back to the community. Being a real estate investor has allowed him the flexibility to work with and fund key charitable projects in Haiti and Mexico. In their desire to give back, Keith and Laura support an orphanage in Haiti, where he helps fund building projects and teaches the local manager to be self-sufficient. Keith also works on projects in Cuba through his church involvement.

Contact Info:
520-222-8657
keith@alliance2911.com

Shannon:
Was there somebody in your life, a mentor, who was in real estate invest-
ing, by chance, that you really thought, "That's who I want to be like?"

Keith:
Yes, there was a gentleman, he unfortunately recently passed, who had a cabin up near ours in Strawberry, Arizona, and his entire retirement was based on 30 to 40 cash flowing rental properties. His son had started his own property management company as a result of them. I said, "You know, that's definitely the way to go because the man doesn't have a financial care in the world, he travels globally on a regular basis, he has time to give back to the community—being his city's man of the year and head of the sister cities program." For him it didn't matter whether the market went up or down because the rental income was always there. That was the inspiration for this move back into real estate. See, I bought my first fourplex when I was 24, but I would get the calls when the heat went off or deal with tough tenants; but he took it to a new level where he could greatly multiply his efforts.

Shannon:
Well, touch on that a little bit for me. You said it doesn't matter whether
or not the market goes up or down. I was about to ask you if you felt like
real estate investing success was contingent on a strong market, but you
just answered that. Explain to me why it doesn't matter if the market
goes up or down.

Keith:
It all depends on your investment strategy and long-term goals. If you're doing one-offs, like a renovation project, wholesaling, or fore-closures, well then, certainly there's a dependence on if the market is hot or not. Our long-term strategy is to buy and hold rental properties that are fully paid. In that case, you're not buying for value, you're buying for cash flow. Under that strategy, cash flow doesn't care whether the house dropped 50,000 in value or went up 25,000. All cash flow cares about is net rental after expenses and management.

Rental rates generally don't go down. If you're in a market where rentals are strong, unless there's something major that happens in that area, for instance a major employer leaves, your rental income is going to be fairly stable. Even then, unfortunately, people will shift to renting as they can't afford the mortgage on their home like they could when they were employed. Conversely, a new employer coming in means people need rental housing for the first year or so while they consider where their "forever home" will be. If you bought correctly, the value of the property doesn't impact your cash flow. So many people get caught up in thinking of the value of a piece of property in a particular market. What I'm concerned with is what, particularly with rental properties, that cash flow will be on a consistent basis. This is also important when analyzing exit strategies for other types of investing such as renovations, etc.

Shannon:

Do I hear you saying it doesn't matter if, say, you bought the property at 300,000 and it drops down to 200,000 in value, as long as you're able to collect a positive cash flow?

Keith:

I would be concerned as to the cause for the drop. If it is macro-market fluctuation, then no. If it is something devastating, like the situation in Flint, Michigan, then no strategy will bring the renters in. However, a rule of thumb is If this is a buy-and-hold property and it's in my portfolio and its purpose is to bring me in monthly cash flow, then value overall doesn't matter. For tax purposes, my accountant would disagree, due to depreciation, but we're discussing cash flow here. The only time it matters is with possible liquidity issues if you see another "bright shiny object" or opportunity where selling would be advantageous. However, that's why we diversify in the markets where we invest.

Shannon:

That makes sense. It sounds like in a down economy, doing a buy-and-hold is a good strategy. What is a good strategy for making money in an up economy?

Keith:

Well, it's interesting, because you can do variations on any of the strategies, in any economy. The deals may be more difficult to find (importance of a good team), and any strategy requires the understanding of and being able to have an exit strategy utilizing one or more of the others. An up economy in one area might be a down economy in another. Nothing limits you geographically with the right teams and right systems in place. In an upswing, you'll focus more at the buying end of the process. In a downswing, you want to be cognizant of the declination in your ARV. Time is not your friend, so don't be chasing the numbers. So when your values are increasing, there is less risk in doing a flip because by the time you're done, there's a high degree of probability of getting your ARV (after repair value) at sale and less fear of those little (issues) that always crop up during demolition. As to the time to buy with holding in mind, well, think of Warren Buffet: **"We simply attempt to be fearful when others are greedy and to be greedy only when others are fearful."** You know, when everybody's running one way, you run the other, so I increase my focus on buy-and-holds as a market heads downward. Don't wait for the "bottom of the market" because you'll never be able to predict it.

Shannon:
Explain to me how important the ARV is. And what are some of the tools that you use or some of the things that you do to help you make sure that you're getting that?

Keith:

ARV is the whole story, isn't it? The key is a concept called "forced appreciation." Can you, through renovation, take a property that was poorly performing in its neighborhood and drive the value to meet the comparables for updated properties? Along with acquisition price, ARV determines if there is enough spread to make the venture worthwhile. We analyze every piece of property, regardless of strategy, i.e., gap funding, buy-and-hold, joint venture, with none of our own funding, with the same type of analysis to develop and achieve the ARV. We use competent real estate professionals; we do comps, and then we double check the comps. The agent also advises on selling trends in such areas as finishes, colors, floorings, layout, etc. When we renovate a house, we want to renovate it to the standards selling in that area. That determines our renovation budget and buyer acceptance. We also look at days on market. It's key to have a high degree of confidence that we're going to be able to carry that property for the time needed to sell. We have a contractor walk the property for a budgetary estimate on repairs. We use a tool that calculates all closing costs and holding costs based on length of project and evaluates several hard money lending options. Then we determine the offer price. We never use the highest ARV in this estimate. If the numbers work, we make an offer. As long as you've got all that in place and you have the amount of money that yields the return to you and/or your investors that you want, then it's a deal worth making an offer on. For an MLS property, the agent will pull comparables on non-renovated properties in the area for a seller reality check validating our offer. We do some private money lending through a self-directed 401(k), and we also invest with our business entity that's outside of our 401(k). This works for us because we can generate far better returns than the company sponsored plans, and we can also generate income for current living.

Shannon:
What do you think is one of the biggest mistakes people make when do-ing a fix-and-flip?

Keith:
Buying with their heart. They buy it as though they're buying their dream house. They watch too many fix-and-flip shows and think the wow factor is everything. Lack of knowledge and the correct appli-cation of that knowledge is the root cause. I know a lot of folks who took a three-day hotel seminar and rather than go on for some form of advanced education, went blindly forward thinking they had all they needed to be successful. They may stumble onto a good deal and make money despite themselves, but what we see in this market,

in Phoenix, is a lot of people buying way over what the price should be for any decent spread and then over-renovating. You can tell the inadequately trained novice investor property because it'll be the most beautiful-looking house on the block, priced way out of the market, and it'll stay there for double or triple the average CDOM. Inevitably you watch the price drop and drop and drop and sadly know they're winding up not making money on the deal or, worse yet, losing the property to their lender. It could have been prevented by something as simple as having a contractor walk the job during due diligence to find the little things your eyes aren't trained to see yet.

Shannon:
Is that similar to when you're buying a car and you do a pre-purchase inspection?

Keith:
Absolutely; it's just basic due diligence and not something a typical home inspection will uncover. When you're renovating and taking a 1960s-era house and converting it up to an open floor plan, you may want to know if you have load-bearing walls you will have to mitigate. You also might want to know if you have plumbing issues that are going to cause you to saw cut concrete to fix sewer issues and if the roof needs replacing. A good contractor can make a fairly general assessment in a walkthrough. It won't be a hard quote but will give you a fair assessment if you have an opportunity or a money-pit. Now despite your best efforts, there will always be a surprise, so you have to allow for that in your calculations as well.

Shannon:
What do you typically budget for surprises?

Keith:
I try and leave about 10 percent of the renovation estimate. So, for instance, on a $45,000 renovation, I try and add another $4,500, just as a gotcha fund.

Shannon:

For a surprise; "bonuses," as we like to call them, right?

Keith:

Exactly. We had a recent project, we knew we had one load-bearing wall but it intersected with another one that we could've sworn was not. We didn't have access to the attic until after we took possession due to the construction. However, you know, we had money in the budget to cover it, and we had a creative contractor who came up with a great solution that didn't cost much money, so we maintained our ROI goals.

Shannon:

Good. You talked about when you got involved in real estate investing you went out and you found the right education, you found the right information so you could make sure that you were doing it right.

Keith:

Right.

Shannon:

Did you find that from a person or a team of people?

Keith:

It was interesting for us because we had gone to a hotel seminar and we found a program we thought was pretty good. My wife was working with the husband of a woman who had done a lot of flips in the San Francisco Bay area. She was on an HGTV series for a while. So we said, "Well, let's take them out to dinner and see if this program's legitimate." We went to dinner and showed her everything, and she's like, "Well, let me tell you what I'm doing." She introduced us to this community of investors, and the thing I liked about the program she was in over the hotel seminar thing is that at the end of the hotel seminar they're gone. There might be a three-day "Boots on the Ground," but after that you're usually left with an 800 number to a mentor and some online education or DVDs.

The difference in this community we're involved with, and the nationwide educational program we have, is that we are constantly surrounded by people who have our back, people with whom we learn and interact. Community is also the best defense against "Lone Wolf Syndrome," where you have the information but never move forward with an actual deal. We are also, in my opinion, the gold standard and can cover any possible real estate type of transaction you would want to do. There is also extensive training on financial literacy. For me, it's taken the fear out of the equation. It's made our ability to get into deals quicker than the other would, had we been on our own.

Shannon:
Nice. What is one of the top real estate strategies that you've learned?

Keith:
Actually, the ability to utilize hard money and private money, to invest in deals that aren't tied to personal credit was a game changer. I didn't know about that aspect of it. The real estate transactions I'd done in the past were all based on my credit, so there were only a certain number I could carry at a time. Using this strategy and using other people's stagnant IRAs to fund deals multiplies the number of projects that I can run concurrently. That's the biggest strategy because it makes all the other strategies work.

Shannon:
But explain it a little bit more to me. You said using other people's money or credit. To me, when I hear that I think, so you just walk up to people and say, "Hey, can I use your credit score to buy a house?"

Keith:
Quite frankly, it is a little of that, but it's not that. You'd be surprised how many people are in situations where they have an old 401(k), IRA, or pension from a former employer. I've heard the figure as high as $25 trillion. When I left my corporate job, I had executive out-placement service as part of my severance. In my networking

sessions, I saw people in a similar situation. They had left one job, looking for another, but now they have a 401(k) they need to roll over. There's a lot of people that have 401s or rollover IRAs that are sitting there just performing at the abysmal rate for mutual funds we're currently seeing.

I love engaging with people. I usually share a little of my story and tell them how I didn't think with my 401(k) there was any way I could ever retire. Then I tell them a bit about taking control of my own finances. They usually have a story to share about what their 401(k) is doing. From there the conversation usually goes to, "Well, if I was able to show you a way that you could earn double or triple what you're earning right now by investing in a project secured by real estate, would you be interested?" Then I show them the numbers on an actual project. With anyone I engage in conversation, I am always prepared to talk concepts. You have to have your act together. It's not just, "Hey, you know, loan me some money." You are always representing your personal brand because you never know when you will run into an investor who will fund your next great opportunity. If they're interested, people say yes or people say, "How do I get involved in doing what you're doing?" It's one of two answers, usually.

Shannon:
Right. When you start talking to people about this and you say, you know, "Would you be interested?" do you always make sure that you have a deal in hand, or do you talk to them beforehand so that you have a next step?

Keith:
No, I talk to them beforehand. That's not to say I may not have a deal, but particularly in our market, once you find a good deal that comes around and you lock it down into a contract, you're there, at least as far as securing the property. You may need a source for earnest money, to go to contract. If you don't lock it down, you're pretty much going to miss the deal, if you locked it down, most of the sellers want to close within 15 days after due diligence. It's good for you to have a list of people that you can call that have already said to you, "Yeah,

I've got the money available." Also, if the money is in a traditional IRA, you need to teach them how to get that into a self-directed plan so that they can access it quicker. That can take several weeks, so it needs some planning.

Shannon:

Got it. You say most of these people want to close within 10 to 15 days. Is that what you'd call a short sale?

Keith:

No, short sales are a completely different thing. It's when a home-owner is wanting to sell his property for less than what he owes the bank and is negotiating with the bank to do that.

The reason for a short closing time, particularly when an investor is buying a property for cash or with hard money from a wholesaler, is they already have the property under contract and are wanting a short closing time to ensure their profit or maximize the profit to the seller. You know, time is money for them, so the longer they're holding the contract, the more it's costing them, so they want a quick close. Or the seller knows they're selling to an investor, and they want to close within 15 days. Also, since they are not waiting for you to get a traditional mortgage, you generally have negotiated a more favorable price. Time may be of the essence for other reasons, such as a pending foreclosure, a divorce, seller moving, etc.

Shannon:

Perfect. With most of your investment partners, do they just invest money or do more people come to you and say, "How can I do what you're doing?"

Keith:

I'm seeing a lot of the latter right now. I've had several people that I've shared what I'm doing and transitioned the conversation from being an investment opportunity to them actually wanting to learn how I got to the point where I'm doing what I do now. Our commu-nity has a process to expand our community and educate investors in our systems because our goal is of course to have more resources and help people. However, if I was to have to put the brakes on my business to help everyone who approaches me, my business would stop, so we have a mechanism to get people to a level of competence where they are talking the same language, can analyze deals, and then partner with us. We've found that has proven successful.

Shannon:

Perfect. I hear you saying you want to mentor people and you want to bring people in; however, you want to continue to do your own thing.

Keith:

Absolutely. Right. If it wasn't for someone taking the time to work with me, I would have never been able to gain the understanding about the projects I am doing now, but that doesn't mean this person is in on every deal with me or that we even have the same strategies long term. I may want to do fix and flips; they may want to concentrate on commercial projects.

Shannon:

Perfect.

Shannon:

Okay. How about multifamily dwellings? Do you dabble in that?

Keith:

We're starting to get into that now. The first property I ever bought was a fourplex. However, in this market, I'm finding that I need to relearn how to properly assess a multi-family project. So I'm actually continuing my education in how to analyze multifamily deals while I'm looking for the right project to come along.

Shannon:

Okay, so I am going to ask you this question then. If someone wanted to invest in multifamily dwellings, what do you think the top three most important things are that they need to know?

Keith:

Well, there are many things that are different in evaluating multi-family dwellings, especially over four units. Anything over four units is generally evaluated using an income capitalization approach vs the comparable approach used in residential purchases. You may be entering the realm of commercial lending and real estate. Also, local regulations differ when you get into larger projects, like common spaces, parking, etc. Tenant regulations may vary. There are significant advantages to investing in multi-family properties in that for one transaction you have multiple doors. There are also creative ways to take a current commercial property, such as an eightplex, and split it into two fours which could take you out of a commercial property and back into residential.

Now, you have some opportunities in rentals that apply even for single-family homes and condos but certainly for multifamily. If you're in an area of town and you can get your property qualified for Section 8 tenants, you can get much higher rental rate per bedroom then you would get in a normal single-family structure rental, so there are big gains to be made there as well. Then we know some folks who are now looking at a 22-door or larger project. That takes on a whole different scope. I'm starting now with finding threes and fours in areas like Miami and Houston, and then go from there.

Shannon:

You've touched several times on property management. Would you want to manage your own properties if you had a fourplex or two or three fourplexes, and wait until you get bigger to hire a property management company? Or do you feel like you should have that from the beginning?

Keith:

No. This is a practice you should start from the beginning. If you truly want to be an investor, then you need to hire professionals with the core competencies that you require. Your focus should be finding good properties, analyzing them, and adding them to your portfolio. You greatly limit yourself if you are also responsible for finding and screening tenants, hiring tradesmen to do repairs, and managing tenant issues and building maintenance. You are responsible for managing the property manager, assuring they are efficiently managing your asset for maximum cash flow. I took care of things myself when I owned my first four-family, and what I found is that it's not fair to you, it's not fair to the tenants. A good property manager is worth their weight in gold; if they are doing their job, you're basically reviewing reports. I also can't personally manage outside my geographical area. I'm not there yet, but my strategy is to invest where the rental market is hot and where I can get the best cash flow, and that may not be in my immediate area. It would be, let's say, ridiculous for me from Phoenix to try and manage a rental property in Indiana. Property management companies earn their keep, and they're typically 10 percent of rents collected. You just figure it into the numbers so it becomes part of the basic math when you're analyzing the deal.

Shannon:

Got it. You were talking about vacancy rate in multifamily. Obviously, your goal is to be 100 percent occupied all the time, but we both know that's not real practical. What is your percentage that you aim for in vacancy rates?

Keith:

It depends; in a good market, what I've seen is you're calculating 5 percent. However, I've seen areas where the vacancy rate runs 15 percent, and that's not a bad thing if the cash flow of the remaining rents support it, if it meets your cash flow target. Again, on a larger project, the vacancy rate is already taken into account with your income analysis approach to valuation. It's a factor that just comes into how the structure of the deal works. For me, if I'm seeing a 15-plus vacancy rate, I've got to question if that's a good rental market or what other mitigating circumstances are there that would still make this viable.

Shannon:

Got it, that makes sense. Is there a question on that list that you wish I would've asked you?

Keith:

I'd really like to touch upon how real estate investing, the way I currently do it, has changed my life. We actually see the ability to have long-term generational income. I did not have a plan that didn't require me to, in order to keep up my lifestyle, sell everything and move to Costa Rica or Ecuador. While that sounds exciting, and I sure hope to have rental properties there among other places, I want to be near family here in Arizona, particularly with a new grandbaby. That was a battle with my wife of 38 years that I was going to lose very quickly. We now have a plan that can get us to where we can now see both. I was on a cruise ship, and though totally relaxing, my business was still working, so it's changed my life to quite a degree.

Shannon:
Nice.

Shannon:
If somebody was going to get started in real estate and they had very little money or poor credit, what are some of the strategies that they could use to get started?

Keith:

Well, you'll hear a lot of people talk about going into wholesaling right away. Wholesaling is the act of doing a lot of legwork and finding the property, getting it under contract, and then finding a cash buyer. In this type of market, cash buyers are everywhere. Finding a deal is what takes a lot of time, so if they have a lot of time and no money, that's a good strategy. But you can also identify people, like we talked about, in your sphere of influence who aren't happy with the performance of their IRA. We show them how to free up that money, and they can invest with you as an equity partner or just as a gap funder, and you can be doing a renovation or a fix-and-flip with none of your own money. I change places between investing my 401(k) funds on some projects and acting as the developer and using someone else's funds on others.

Shannon:
How do you make sure that it is "fair" to you if it's your money and your partner has no money in it? How is that fair?

Keith:
Well, there's the split of responsibilities. As the funder, I get a yea or nay on decisions, but he or she, depending on who the partner is, will be responsible for managing the contractor. They're responsible for basically the project management end, working with the realtor to market it, making sure everything is on time and on schedule. That's their role. They secure the hard money loan and make sure that the payments are made. My role, even though there might be an equity split, is more advise and consent, and providing the gap funding.

Shannon:
Would you consider that almost like an operating partner, or would you consider it more as an administrative partner?

Keith:
We view them generally as an operating partner. There are at least two ways to structure a deal, depending on the source of funds you are using for the gap. I could just gap fund the project for a set rate of interest, and then it's their project and I get my interest rate and I'm happy with it. When I've chosen to do an equity partnership, it's because I see a potential for a bigger upside, and so I'm a little bit more active in the decision process. I'm actually on the title, second position lien holder, and I have a joint venture agreement with the person identifying roles and responsibilities. The upside to that, if we hit our ARVs and keep in budget, can be substantially higher than the flat rate of interest that is charged as a gap funder.

Shannon:
Perfect. You keep saying "gap funder." What is that?

Keith:
It's when you deal with hard money loans. For those people who don't

understand investments, a regular home loan through a bank, which does not fit our business model, but if you're doing a home loan through a bank, they're not going to loan you 100 percent. They're going to loan you 80 percent, and you've got to come up with 20 percent now. So think of it that way. A typical hard money lender bases the loan decision on the property alone. Most do not do a credit check or verify income. They look at the numbers you're giving them on the deal and they verify your comps and they say, "All right, we'll loan 80 percent of the purchase price and 80 percent of the rehabilitation cost." So the gap funder comes up with the 20 percent for the purchase, 20 percent for the rehabilitation, and the closing cost or carrying cost to get the project through to completion. That funding closes the gap between the hard money lender and what it takes to complete the project.

Shannon:
Sometimes we have opinions on things, but they're more factual. How has it changed your life?

Keith:
Before we move on to that, Shannon, there was one other thing when talking about fear. Back in 2002, I think I still have them around some-where, I bought the "Carlton Sheets" books and tapes, and I ordered so many real estate packages off of infomercials and did nothing with them. There was always that sense of, what if I screw up? What if I fail at this? Now, I'm generally not risk averse. I've built homes on spec in New Jersey in the 80s, I've owned my own companies as an entrepreneur, but I never got beyond what I call the retail approach to real estate. We sat in a hotel seminar and could have pulled the trigger several times, but it was fear that held us back. What I came to realize is what is the alternative, you know? Fear is just nothing more than lack of knowledge and lack of education. We use a lot of things to hold us back, and for me, once you make the commitment, fear seems to go away.

In fact, aside from my life verse which is Jeremiah 29:11, which para-phrases as, "I know the plans I have for you declares the Lord. Plans to prosper you and not to harm you. Plans for a future," there is one quote I would like to leave for those standing on the precipice of this real estate experience. It is from the Scottish Himalayan Expedition:

"Until one is committed there is hesitancy, the chance to draw back, always ineffectiveness. Concerning all acts of initiative (and creation), there is one elementary truth, the ignorance of which kills countless ideas and splendid plans: that the moment one definitely commits oneself, then Providence moves too. All sorts of things occur to help one that would never otherwise have occurred. A whole stream of events issues from the decision, raising in one's favour all manner of unforeseen incidents and meetings and material assistance, which no man could have dreamt would have come his way. I have learned a deep respect for one of Goethe's couplets: 'Whatever you can do, or dream you can, begin it. Boldness has genius, power, and magic in it." —W. H. Murray (J. M. Dent & Sons Ltd., 1951)

This is what we've seen happen in our lives; once we took that step, the things that came into our lives we could've never imagined. Paying it forward and helping others is a big part of who my wife and I are as well.

Shannon:
Okay, well I love that you answered the fear question. Sorry I didn't ask you that one. I just thought, you know, "He doesn't sound like he had any fear coming in." It's amazing, the assumptions that we make that we probably shouldn't have, so thank you for that.

Keith:
Yeah, at the hotel seminar, I held back because of fear, and probably good thing, because I wouldn't't've had the community I have now.

Shannon:
Right, aren't you glad that you did?

Keith:
Certainly, you know, we were given that gift of fear for a reason, so sometimes fear is fear and sometimes it's an appropriate response because there is something better around the corner, or something is trying to eat you!

Shannon:
What is your legacy that you'd like to leave behind?

Keith:
Well, that's a good question for me because I have always tried to be of service to people. As a teen, I worked with the Christian Appalachian Project in the mountains of Kentucky. I was a camp counselor for MDAA. We've tried to instill those values in our children and feel we have raised boys that have an appreciation of their duty to pay it forward. We fund an orphanage in Haiti, helping them secure their building. We've also been active in projects in Mexico, Cuba, and in the States. I also mentor in my Global Supply Chain Consulting business, helping start-ups obtain funding. So being involved in an investment group where "pay it forward" is rooted in their DNA was a natural for us. I've heard it said that you can't receive if your hand is closed. My children are following in the same vein, so I guess in the important matters, that is my legacy. Financially, I would like to be at the point where my assets remain in a family 'office' that future generations can contribute to and benefit from. I'm a ways off from that, but with the systems at my disposal, it is at least on the horizon.

What is truly exciting about the way we approach our business, through our network now, is that it is truly synergistic with the rest of our plans. It is fundamentally the same: helping people with real estate challenges, educating them, and providing a way out of their predicament. We are also helping to influence other like-minded entrepreneurs to achieve success in real estate and financial literacy. You just naturally want to share what you learn with other people so they can experience the same rewards you have. I can't think of a better legacy than that. We may not move the needle on a global level, but in our little corner of the universe we can make a difference.

David & Gilda Couzins

David Couzins grew up on multiple Strategic Air Command bases during the second half of the Cold War. He enlisted as an infantryman in the US Army in 1982 and participated in combat training and security operations throughout the Hawaiian Islands, the Philippines, and Australia. After receiving his honorable discharge, David worked in several of the nation's largest international law firms, building and managing computer technology departments staffed by litigation support professionals who provided legal teams in the United States and Europe with electronic discovery consulting and database support services.

Fifteen years ago, at the urging of his wife, Gilda, David established D&G Real Estate Corporation in the Chicago suburbs and became a managing broker licensed by the State of Illinois.

David also has a passion for writing fiction and in 2010 published his first novel: *Domers* (www.domersbook.com) which follows the adventures of a young couple struggling to cope with an American landscape alien to them, aided by newfound friends, all against the backdrop of a looming war.

Gilda Couzins is the third of seven children who were born in the Philippines to a poor fisherman/farmer and his wife. Beyond the white sandy shore that was Gilda's front yard, numerous tiny trop-ical islands sat scattered across a calm, crystal blue ocean. In her backyard rose a mountain covered in lush green tropical forest. This was the place Gilda called her Paradise.

But it wasn't only warm, natural beauty that surrounded Gilda's modest home—poverty was ever-present as well. Gilda was told by many of the local villagers—friends and family—that she would not get very far in life, nor would she have a chance at a good education because her parents couldn't even provide enough food for her and her siblings to eat. They said she should expect to be married early and to have children before leaving high school.

But those dire predictions did not stop Gilda from dreaming big.

At the age of five, Gilda began selling fish in the nearby villages to help her parents with living expenses. In first grade, she made coconut candies and rice cakes to sell to her classmates and teachers so that she could buy her own books and school supplies. After graduating high school, Gilda left her home and traveled to a neighboring island to attend the Philippine Air Force college earning a Bachelor's degree in Accounting while working full time in the school's accounting office, which allowed her to get free tuition, books, and room and board.

While still attending college, Gilda continued to hone her entre-preneurial skills by selling food items in the school canteen as well as household goods—sometimes on an installment basis—all of which allowed her to graduate college without requiring any finan-cial support from her family.

Soon after graduation in 1988, Gilda married David and immi-grated to the United States where she is now a citizen. Within months of arriving in the eastern US, Gilda and David signed a contract on a two-bedroom condo financed with a VA loan, and thus began her adventures in the world of real estate. Gilda now lives with David, their three boys—Kevin, Nathan, and Jonathan—and her parents in the suburbs of Chicago.

Throughout the past 25 years, Gilda has had a number of jobs in the financial industry, and she is an experienced mortgage loan officer. During that span, Gilda and her husband continued to invest in real estate, acquiring 15 properties and building a church in Gilda's home town. Gilda is looking to accelerate her real estate investing activities and is exposing her three sons to the excellent opportunities that a career in real estate investing provides.

Gilda is grateful to her whole family and her husband's family for all their help and support, and above all, she is grateful to our God the Father, the Son, and the Holy Spirit for guiding and helping her in everything.

Shannon:

So, what inspired the two of you to get into real estate investing?

Gilda:

For us, everything started 29 years ago when we first got married. Dave had an apartment, but I knew that paying rent wasn't the way to build wealth. We didn't have much money when we were starting out, so we used Dave's status as a military veteran to get a VA loan to purchase a 1,000-square foot condo. That's where it all started. We have been buying properties ever since. We have acquired 15 properties and have sold 2. We even built a church in my home town in 2002—that was a very fun and fulfilling experience.

We have always looked at real estate investing as a great way to build for retirement, as well as to create a legacy to pass along to kids and grandkids someday, so they can get a head start in life and not have to struggle as much as Dave and I did.

Shannon:

Okay. So you've kind of always been in real estate investing.

Gilda:

Yes, absolutely.

Shannon:

So why did you decide to get educated if you're already successful? You already have 13 properties.

Gilda:

Ah, that's an easy one. In 2006, we found a nice single-family house in a new neighborhood in a fast-growing area of the country. We thought this would be a great investment property—how could we miss? Of course, now we know that we had just purchased a property at the height of the real estate bubble and things would soon collapse. We were stuck with an expensive, over-inflated property that had an upside-down mortgage for years. We eventually sold the house, but at a $200,000 loss. That hurt. Clearly, we didn't know it all and we had to fill in some gaps in our education if we were to prevent repeating that disaster.

Coincidentally, we stumbled onto a great real estate education system while I was out interviewing hard money lenders to fund a small, $75,000 mixed-use commercial property that I had under contract. I was invited to a meeting of local real estate investors and business professionals where I learned the important concept: "I don't know what I don't know," and I had better beef up my real estate education to both avoid costly errors and to expand the number of real estate investing strategies in my investing toolbox. Having knowledge of multiple real estate strategies—instead of merely one or two—is a great way to mitigate risk. I now know that for every real estate deal I work, I should have three exit strategies in place. If we had paid more attention to our real estate investing education, Dave and I wouldn't have taken that large loss.

Shannon:
Right.

Gilda:
So, education makes a big difference.

David:
Exactly. Once Gilda got into that real estate education, and we started immersing ourselves in that education, we realized more and more that there were many concepts with which we had no familiarity— things that we just never knew. So, the education opened our eyes to many more possibilities and now we're discovering all kinds of new

ways to do real estate investing. We're very excited to try out these additional strategies, and in fact, we're already doing that.

Shannon:

So, David, tell me… Gilda went to the class. Did you go with her?

David:

No, I didn't. Gilda was the one who initiated our re-education process, and she spent a good amount of time—many months—checking things out to make sure this was truly a good opportunity that would help our business. I work in a large national law firm in downtown Chicago, so I just didn't have as much time to vet various education opportunities.

Gilda:

Seven months of vetting before we went forward with that particular real estate investing education opportunity.

David:

Right. Gilda realized what a great opportunity it was, and after a few months of due diligence, she asked me to come down and see for myself what this was all about.

Shannon:

That's what I was going to ask—how did that conversation go? Did you say, "Mm, no," or were you like, "Absolutely, Gilda, I'm in."

Gilda:

Actually, it was kind of funny… because I had no idea what kind of meeting I was sitting in on that Thursday evening. I went by myself, and then I came home that night all excited because Dave and I already had plans for how to expand our business, but we didn't have the required "systems" developed yet. I told him, "I just sat in on a meeting of a group that already had business systems built and was dedicated to helping others use those systems to build their real estate businesses."

So that was great, but Dave didn't jump in immediately. Back in 2013, after we took that large loss on the one property, Dave told me,

"Honey, no more real estate." But I just told him, "Honey, if we stop now, we'll never recover any of that money. The only way for us to recover that money is to keep going forward and not stopping. But we just have to, you know, do it smarter by better educating ourselves."

David:

And Gilda had more time to initiate our business improvement program because, as I mentioned earlier, I have a job, a W2 job that keeps me busy not just 40 hours a week but sometimes 60, 70, 80 hours a week. So I'm spending a lot of my time with that. And part of the reason for moving into real estate investing is because I want to get away from that W2 job. Real estate investing is so much more rewarding and profitable than getting up at 5:30 every morning, commuting two hours to Chicago, working all day, and then commuting two hours back. So much of my day is just gone.

Shannon:
Right. So, David, tell me, so far, what is the top real estate strategy that you have learned?

David:

Well, I would say the lease option. And I'm learning that, again, through Gilda because she's going down and attending these classes, and she's giving me a briefing on what she's learned. I am amazed at the power of the lease option because you can control a lot of real estate without having to come up with a lot of your own money.

Shannon:
Okay. Gilda, do you want to expand on that?

Gilda:

Yes, yes. Our ultimate goal is to have a significant number of rentals. The buy and hold strategy, that's really our ultimate plan, and maybe being a bank—a lender that is—so we can help people with their financing as well. I know and have learned a number of investing strategies now, and Dave is correct, the lease option is a particularly attractive strategy, and we are pursuing option opportunities right now.

David:

That's because the lease option strategy works well for people who don't have good credit or who can't buy a house the usual way—getting a mortgage from a bank. We can help people move into houses with lease options where they otherwise couldn't get into a house the traditional way because they don't qualify for bank loans.

Shannon:

So, it sounds like a lease option is a great strategy for someone who's starting with little money or poor credit, is that correct?

Gilda:

Yes, that's correct. And there are other real estate strategies that don't require much in the way of start-up capital. Wholesaling, for example, is probably even better for new investors or investors with little capital. The returns aren't as high but neither are the risks. So it's a great way to get your feet wet in the investing arena. And you can pair up with other people who have resources that you don't have.

Also, I have many years of experience in the mortgage industry and I often advise others on the importance of fixing their credit, building their credit, and building their corporate and personal lines of credit to gain access to capital for their businesses.

Shannon:

Right. So Gilda, you actually talked about wholesaling.

Gilda:

Yes.

Shannon:

What is wholesaling?

Gilda:

Wholesaling is basically gaining temporary control of a property by putting it under contract with the intention of selling that contract to an investor for a wholesaling fee. So you do the legwork of finding a good investment property, then you put that property in front of an investor. Many investors are happy to pay the wholesaler what is in essence a finder's fee for doing the research and analysis that brings a good deal to the investor—who didn't have to spend his or her own time searching for investments.

Shannon:

Okay. How do you find a wholesale property?

Gilda:

There are many ways to find a property to wholesale, such as through your personal and professional networks, searching probate records, advertisements, bankruptcy or foreclosure notices, real estate brokers, driving neighborhoods for "For Sale By Owner" properties… there are many ways.

David:

Right, and keep in mind that there's less competition for properties that are not on the market yet. You can certainly find some good deals on a multiple listing service, but higher profits flow more often from unlisted properties.

We're also getting our kids involved, and they are beginning to learn about real estate investing as well. We have three boys, ages 24, 19, and 16. Our younger two have a goal of finding a rental property within a year—so they are out there helping to find properties as well.

Shannon:

Nice.

Gilda:

It's pretty exciting to do this business as a family.

Shannon:

Let's elaborate on the whole family thing here, where you've got the 16 and 19 year old. Where are they going to look? And when you say they want to acquire a property, how are they doing it so young?

Gilda:

Right.

Shannon:

So are they going down to the courthouse? Are they searching on Zillow? Are they looking for homes with dead grass?

Gilda:

Well, we've actually started bringing them to property tours. They are learning how to evaluate property, learning things like rehab costs, holding costs, after repair values, financing costs, calculating profit, etc.

They come to our workshops and marketing meetings and are discovering for themselves that real estate investing is full of great opportunities. They are getting really excited about it actually and are already talking about doing their own deals to help with funding college.

Shannon:

Right, so it sounds like you guys understand that, in your real estate investing career, you really need a strong team. And you're building your family team, which is huge because family adds that extra element of trust immediately. How important is it for you to establish a team outside of your family to help you be successful?

Gilda:

Having a team is critically important because we can't do this on our own. Real estate deals require legal professionals, accounting professionals, contractors, title companies, inspectors, appraisers, etc. The more people on your team, the more properties you can flip, or rent, or lease option.

Shannon:

Great. So, Gilda, you said that you are a mortgage loan officer, is that correct?

Gilda:

Yes, I have been a mortgage loan officer since 2003. I also have a Bachelor's degree in Accounting.

Shannon:

Okay, so you know all about the economy.

Gilda:

Yes, yes.

Shannon:

Strong economies, weak economies...

Gilda:

Up, down, right.

Shannon:

Do you feel like real estate investing success is dependent upon a strong economy?

Gilda:

No, not really. It's all about knowledge. If you have the knowledge of multiple real estate strategies, you can invest in real estate no matter what the economy is doing. Some strategies work well in a booming economy; other strategies are more suited to declining economies. As always, education is the key to minimizing risk whether you are working a booming or busting economy.

Shannon:

So what's one strategy that you can use in a market that's going up?

David:

The fix and flip works well in a booming economy because more people can afford to buy, housing inventories are lower, and properties are appreciating in value, so your risks of getting stuck with a non-performing property are lower. Of course, if the economy is tanking, the fix and flip strategy will have more risk attached to it— fewer people are in the market for purchasing, property values are declining.

Gilda:

Right.

David:

Also, if the economy is declining, the buy and hold strategy becomes more popular as you generate rental income to cover your holding costs (such as mortgage principle and interest and real estate taxes) and make positive cash flow. You might not be gaining much equity on the appreciation of your real estate, but you are making passive income from the real estate that you're holding.

Shannon:

What is passive income, David?

David:

The simplest way to describe passive income is—it's when your money works for you instead of you working for your money. It's income that you receive without having to do the work yourself. If you own rental properties, you have tenants living in those rental properties, and they're paying you the rent. You're not getting out, commuting to an office, and working at a W-2 day-job for a boss. Your money is working for you, and others are giving you the income. So passive income just rolls in whether you get out of bed or not—I like that concept!

Shannon:

Well it sounds like I would much rather make passive income sitting on my couch...

David:

That's exactly right, and that's the power of real estate.

Gilda:

There are other forms of passive income out there as well, but one of the things that we love about real estate is that you can generate income and at the same time give some people a place to live while giving others employment. It's particularly rewarding when you can use an investing strategy like lease options to put someone into a home that they otherwise wouldn't be able to get into.

Shannon:

Gilda, you had touched on a positive cash flow. Does that have something to do with passive income? Do passive income and cash flow go together?

Gilda:

Oh, yes. In real estate investing, cash flow is king. When you invest in a rental property, you need your passive income—the rent— to give you a positive cash flow. Meaning the monthly rent covers your monthly expenses and includes some profit margin as well. For example, if I'm renting a property for $1,500 but my monthly expenses are $1000, then I have a positive cash flow of $500.

David:

Right, you have somebody else paying you so that you can pay your own mortgage. And the leftover is the positive cash flow that you can use to do other things—our favorite 'other thing' being investing in more real estate.

Shannon:

Awesome. So do you guys have a goal? I know you said both of your sons have a goal to have one property. Do you guys have both a short-term and a long-term goal? So that, David, you can get out of your W2 job that you are speaking about, so you won't do that commute. Do you have a "when we hit this number, David will quit his job"?

David:

Yes, our short-term goal is to generate around $20,000 in positive cash flow per month. Once we hit that, then I'm going to say 'goodbye' to my day job. Again, that's the short-term goal, so we won't stop there. Once I'm out of that W2 job, I will have all those hours to devote to our real estate investing operations and that is going to greatly accelerate what we're already doing. Our business will really be growing exponentially at that point.

Shannon:

So, do you guys foresee all of this being in residential property, single family? Or do you foresee multi-family or commercial real estate in your future?

Gilda:

All of the above! Long term, we plan to diversify and invest in multiple types of real estate. We already have single family, condo, and commercial real estate in our portfolio. At the moment, we're focusing more on single-family properties, but we're also beginning to keep an eye out for multi-family properties. You always want to be open to good opportunities whenever you come across them—even if those opportunities aren't necessarily in your current comfort zone. It's those opportunities that lead you to take on more challenges and expand your business beyond anything you actively planned for.

Shannon:

Why do you feel that it's important to diversify?

Gilda:

Diversity in your portfolio is great because it can be helpful when negotiating the ups and downs of economic and real estate cycles, but it's not a requirement. A person can specialize in a specific type of property and a specific real estate strategy, and their experience over time in that field will give them the expertise to prosper in any economy. However, I also personally prefer diversity because it's just more fun and challenging. I haven't done any tax liens yet, but that looks like a strategy I want to dive into.

David:

Yes, the economy invariably has ups and downs, up and down cycles and nothing's going to change that—that's just a fact of life. If you diversify and employ multiple strategies, you'll be well-positioned to ride those up and down cycles and stay afloat and not have a crash.

Shannon:

So, kind of, to avoid the situation that you fell into recently.

David:

That's exactly right. We didn't have the knowledge back then, but we have learned a lot about real estate investing since then.

Shannon:

Isn't it great to learn things that you don't even know... have answers to questions that you don't even know you should be asking?

David:

Yes, absolutely.

Gilda:

Yes and yes!

Shannon:

Perfect. So, Gilda, you actually mentioned tax liens.

Gilda:

Right.

Shannon:

Tell me how a real estate investor can benefit from a tax lien. What is that?

Gilda:

Sure, a tax lien happens when people don't pay the local real estate taxes on property they own. Their county of residence—usually through the county assessor's office—will impose a tax lien on the property, and then if the property owner doesn't pay the taxes due, the county will sell those liens to investors through a public auction. If the property owner doesn't pay the tax due plus interest and fees during the redemption period, then the investor gets the property. If, however, the property owner does pay off the tax lien, then the investor recovers his investment plus interest (up to 18 percent in Cook County, Illinois). The exact return depends on what state the property is in.

Shannon:

Okay, so elaborate on the tax lien. What you said was that the county will put a lien on it, and then anybody can buy it. So how do you know that a tax lien is there, and how do you go about buying it? You make it sound so simple, yet, if everybody knew these tax liens were out there, and you could buy them and make 18 percent on your money in six months to two years, that's a pretty good return on investment.

Gilda:

Yes, it is a good return, and now you see how a real estate investing education pays great dividends.

Tax liens are published by the county assessor's office in local newspapers and websites and are often put into binders kept in the assessor's office for the public to review. Often, the tax lien sales only occur on a specific day of the year set by the assessor's office, and methods of payment can differ by jurisdiction, so you have to do some research on procedure in the county you are interested in. And, of course, you do some leg work to gather as much information about the property as you can. You don't want to get stuck with a dud property that you can't sell and have to start paying taxes on yourself!

Shannon:

Can you just walk down there with a check or a credit card and say, "I wanna buy this?"

Gilda:

Tax lien sales are fully open to the public in a proceeding called a "tax-defaulted property auction," so you will likely be in a bidding situation. But I can't emphasize enough: long before you show up at the assessor's office to bid on tax liens, you must have done your due diligence on the properties in which you are interested. And as I mentioned earlier, you will need to have done your procedure research for the particular county, including methods of payment.

Shannon:

Great. David, do you have anything you'd like to add to that?

David:

No. That covers it for me.

Shannon:

Okay. So I'm going to ask you guys the last official question, and you've actually already touched on it a little bit. But I want to ask officially, and then you guys can ask me questions.

So the last official question, and David, I'm going to start with you on this, is what type of legacy do you want to leave? And before you answer this, where you guys have already touched on it is where you want to be able to leave financial stability behind for your children and, eventually, grandchildren. But I want you to kind of think more of, "If I got to be a fly on the wall at my own funeral, what do I want people to be saying about me? What's the legacy that I want people to remember me by?"

David:

Well, I'd hope that I was able to not just generate wealth for myself but to help others do the same. Hopefully help family, friends, and friends of friends do the same. I want to pass along things I've learned so that they can create wealth and live a better life. I have learned that some of the education we acquire through life just isn't designed to awaken the full potential we have inside of us. We must become responsible for our own education and not leave that important task for others to dictate what we learn and what we don't.

Shannon:

What type of legacy do you want to leave?

Gilda:

Well, I'd like for people to remember me for my "why." Why do we get up in the morning? Because of our kids, our family, and our desire to help other people. I said that back in 2002; we built a church. We're Christians, so we believe in heaven. We would like to help people not only to be able to acquire wealth but to live well and be happy and to pass down happiness to kids, grandkids, and future generations. Saving souls is more important than saving money.

Giving back to the community around us is important. We have a foundation that we opened to help with emergency food for the elderly. Right now it's still kind of in a pilot study because we don't have the 501(c) designation yet, but that is one of our goals. And that's something that I would like to be able to expand, hopefully sooner than later, and be able to help a lot of people not only in this country but also in different countries.

And any legacy we leave, we are training our kids to pick it up, carry it, and built on it so that they too can keep it going in perpetual motion. Nobody wants a stagnant, moldy legacy!

Dr. Ram Mishra

Dr. Ram Mishra is the Founder and CEO of Senior Care Living, Agency Manager of Acquire Financial Solutions, and an avid real estate investor who created and controls multiple corporations for his real estate developments and rental portfolio.

Born and raised in Grand Rapids, MI, Ram went to India for medical school, and graduated in 2004 with a Bachelors in Medicine & Surgery. When Ram came back to Michigan, he decided to pursue a Masters in Hospital Administration from Grand Valley State University in Michigan. While taking his classes, Ram started working as a loan officer at a small mortgage brokerage where he would begin his financial and entrepreneurial journey. Shortly after, he also became a Licensed Life Insurance Agent, created Acquire Financial Solutions. and started helping protect families with Insurance and Financial Services.

In 2008, Ram and his family moved to Brooklyn, NY where he for several mortgage companies in New York City during the recession. By 2011, he felt the insecurity of corporate jobs, decided he wanted to be his own boss, and become a real estate investor and developer. He started getting educated, building his team, acquired his first duplex in NYC with just $500 down. Since 2011, Ram has been helping people protect themselves with personal insurance, helping people learn the power of creating wealth through real estate investing while at the same time developing his real estate business, building his rental portfolio and senior care business. Ram also enjoys spending time with family and friends, travelling the world, and is committed to helping people better their lives.

Contact Info:
RamjiMishra.com

Shannon:
What inspired you to get into real estate investing?

Ram:
For me it was more of an accident...after completing medical school in India, my wife and I came back to the US, we started applying for jobs, and every position we applied for was filled or they said we were too over qualified. Frustrated with my search, I stumbled on an ad recruiting for mortgage loan officers, so I applied and started working for a local mortgage company in Grand Rapids. After originating my first mortgage, I started marketing for more clients, and it turned out one of my clients was a real estate investor who controlled hundreds of properties in the Grand Rapids area, and he asked me if I could work with his buyers and get them financed out of their land contracts. So was mind blowing for me when I saw the number of properties he owned.

I started researching more how to get into real estate online, went to a few guru seminars, started going to every real estate event I could find, and finally started my training in 2011, and my training was an eye opener as I spent my whole life learning medicine, and nothing about real estate or finance, and that's when I decided I want to pursue my career as a real estate investor.

Shannon:

Thank you. According to Forbes magazine, real estate is one of the top three ways people become wealthy. As a real estate expert, why do you think this is the case?

Ram:

We all need three things to survive in this world. Food, Water & Shelter. With a population boom going on and for the common person, shelter or real estate is one of the few things that we can leverage and actually invest in. Once you acquire real estate, you can see it, feel it, touch it, fix it up, and you can sell it for a profit or rent it out for income, potentially income for life, plus get tax deductions. We can't go to the bank and ask to buy Apple or Microsoft at a discounted price or with let's say 5-10% down. Real estate is only investment I know of which can be leveraged for little to no money, and there's so many lenders out there willing to lend on real estate. With a population boom happening around the world, real estate is definitely one of the top ways to create wealth.

Shannon:

How does your education in real estate change the way that you invest?

Ram:

Before getting educated, I wanted to get into wholesaling and fix and flips because that's what is promoted. When you turn the TV or radio, somebody's advertising about fixing and flipping event or they're selling a course on wholesaling.

Education has dramatically changed the way I invest, changed me from having that 'employee' mentality into having an entrepreneurial mentality. I am a student for life. After enrolling my training and going through all of the different 50+ classes, I'm became so much more knowledgeable, open minded, more creative when I'm structuring a real estate transaction. Most importantly I'm now much more in-tune with my finances, and my personal business plan for my family's legacy. Being educated and having the knowledge really gives you that power over other novice investors, and I'm continuously getting educated.

Shannon:

What is one of the top real estate strategies that you have learned?

Ram:

Buy and hold is by far the top real estate strategy that I've concentrated on. As I said before, I wanted to do fix and flips and wholesaling, even my first property in Brooklyn, NY, I thought I would wholesale or fix and flip it for quick cash as we were living paycheck to paycheck. I had just started my training in August of 2011, going through my buy and hold, more specifically lease option and subject to classes, and with a little help from my team, I put everything together, acquired the property with just $500 on a lease option in Sept 2011. By 2013, I exercised the option to purchase the property which wasn't possible for us in 2011. Now, 7rs later we still own that property today with positive cash flow and a ton of equity. After that 1st transaction, we've been able to acquire multiple properties using the same strategy.

Shannon:

What are some creative ways that you have acquired a property?

Ram:

Lease options, joint partnerships, and subject to and seller financing are the main strategies I've used so far. Lease options and seller financing are great strategies. They were advertised more like rent to own, or land contracts, but the rules have changed on land contracts, so most investors stick to lease options or seller financing. There are multiple ways that a lease option can be structured, and it's a great strategy for both buyers and sellers. Seller financing or owner financing is also similar to doing a land contract. If you can show an owner how to be the bank, they may agree to let you acquire the property with little to no money down, and you can pay the seller monthly payments just like you would to the bank.

A subject too, is where the seller transfers the mortgage to the buyer. On top of that we've done private money, hard money, we've used traditional bank financing. I have made a few friends networking that partnered up with hedge funds to get funding for their fix and flip business. So, there's a lot of creative ways to go out there and do real estate without using your own money, just make sure you use an attorney and/or professional to make sure your contract or agreement is good.

Shannon:
You touched on several different things, but one of the things that you specifically said was land contract. What is that?

Ram:
A land contract is a form of seller financing, similar to a mortgage, but instead the buyer makes payments to the owner (seller) until the price is paid in full. Each state will have different laws, so it's important an attorney is used to make sure that the contract is legal to prevent disputes down the road. There have a lot of problems with land contracts, as some real estate investors would buy cheap property and sell it to anyone with a heartbeat, with $1,000 or $2,000 down. Many contracts had balloon payments and a lot of the buyers were not given proper financial or credit counseling, homes were sold to them in disrepair, and in turn a lot of those buyers lost their down payment, and would have to find a different home to rent or purchase. So, a lot of laws have changed for the better, but whether you want to do seller financing, a land contract or a lease option, I would recommend using an attorney who knows what they are doing.

Shannon:
What would you say is the number one mistake an individual makes when buying their first investment property?

Ram:
I would say jumping into the deal before running their numbers which I've seen a lot of. During the six years when I was living in New York, people would come to me saying "Ram, so and so agent or wholesaler is telling me this is a good deal. I'm racing to put the down payment on it" And I've seen people make that mistake just because a professional or an agent or broker said, "Oh this is a really good deal, you should get it." The new investor doesn't do their due dili-

gence, they don't run their numbers properly. They don't fully take into account what are their resources, acquisition, holding, repair or selling costs. So really, they need to take time to analyze the deal. They shouldn't overlook a lot of those small things that could potentially cost a lot of money in the long run. It's very easy to lose $20,000, $40,000 in a real estate deal if you don't take your time and do your due diligence when you're buying your first property.

Shannon:

It almost sounds like you were mentoring them, is that an accurate statement?

Ram:

Yes, I like to help new investors, just like my mentor who helped me with my 1st deal in Brooklyn and still helps me to this day. I love to attend networking events, and I started to host my own networking meetings, and group trainings to get to know more people and to give back to my community. These meetings have allowed me to meet new investors who I'm happy to help and I've even met a few new mentors that have helped me dramatically with my business.

Shannon:

That is very true, isn't it? How have mentors in your real estate investing helped you to navigate potential pitfalls?

Ram:

Yes, my mentor slowed me down, asked me a lot of questions which forced me to go through my training again and again, and he basically helped guide me to structure my first creative transaction (a lease option), helped me plan the rehab, and we I still own that property in New York City today. I basically wrote the contract myself, my mentor reviewed it for me, they my attorney reviewed it, then I gave it to the seller's attorney. When the seller's attorney had a problem, my mentor got on the phone and helped me out. So, if you have the right mentor, that mentor can go a long way. If it wasn't for him, I would have likely wholesaled it and instead that transaction was much, much more profitable and we still own that property. He's also been very instrumental in structuring some bigger transactions with 33 properties, another had about 60 properties, and another deal with close to over 100 properties. Being able to be a part of these advanced transactions really inspired me to move my business forward. So, it's very important that you network and have not just one mentor, but have multiple mentors that you can go to.

Shannon:
Can you explain how you all worked on so many properties at once.

Ram:
Sure, it's all about having a good team, and it helps that my mentor has been in the business much longer than me. Many times, he gets called when other real estate investors have trouble managing their portfolio, or maybe they are aged or getting old so they cannot manage their portfolios anymore. Many of these transactions were also supervised with help from CPA's and Attorneys and other real estate investors part of our team, so we had a great team partners and professionals ready to work with us.

Shannon:
In your business, how do you help others learn more about real estate?

Ram:
Besides attending local meetings, I also host my own networking events like cash flow games, real estate workshops where new investors can come and discuss real estate deals. We meet new investors almost every week so, it's nice to be able to work with other people. I introduce many to the educational system that got me involved. Once people have that basic knowledge then we'll even go out there and we will partner with new investors, whether it could be a fix and flip or a buy and hold, but the number one way I help other is through making sure that people are educated.

Shannon:
What is cash flow, and why is it so important?

Ram:

In real estate investing, cash flow is basically what's left over from your rent payments. Gross revenue minus your expenses = your net income. Cash Flow is the lifeblood of every business. If you don't have cash flow coming into your business then your business is going to die. So, it's important to be able to generate multiple income streams so if one cash flow stream goes out, you still have other cash flow streams. This is very important with buy and hold real estate investing... especially if you own properties in a lot of different areas, vacancy rates can fluctuate so I believe it's vital to have different types of cash flowing real estate. For instance, multi-families, mobile homes, storage units, single family homes, the list can go on, but any type of real estate asset which can provide you regular income.

Shannon:

It does. Do you feel that real estate investing is dependent upon a strong economy?

Ram:

No. Obviously in a strong economy, real estate usually thrives. But if you have a big rental portfolio in one city, which maybe thrives on the auto industry like Detroit, and all of sudden the market crashes, jobs are gone, you get a bunch of empty houses ready to go into foreclosure if you cannot maintain them. On the flip side, in a down economy, that might be the ideal place to acquire property at a significant discount through foreclosures, short sales, REO's. A good investor should be able to study the markets before investing in a particular area and be able to weather through almost any economy whether weak or strong.

Shannon:

What is a good investment strategy for an up economy? You touched a little bit on what's good for a down economy, but what's good for an up economy?

Ram:

For an up economy, Fix and Flips, Buy and hold, Single Family rentals, Multi units, Commercial properties, any type of property that cash flows are usually great investments in an up economy. Yes, we did have a crash and there were a lot of things that led to the crash, but with the population explosion that we're having, it's probably going to be a long time before you see another crash like what we experienced, but it will happen somewhere. There are so many different uses for real estate which cash flow, multifamily developments, hotels, student housing, senior care, storage units on vacant land. You also will see investors create housing and office spaces out of vacant commercial properties and there will be land development. In any strong economy, there's development, job creation, an influx of people who are going to need homes.

Shannon:
You touched a little bit on multi family. If someone wanted to invest in multi-family units, what advice would you give them?

Ram:
Make sure that you have your team, when you find your property, inspect and analyze it properly. It doesn't matter what type of real estate deal that you're doing, using your team is very important whether you're investing in a single family or multi-families, but acquiring one 10-unit home is definitely a lot easier than buying 10 separate homes. There are also easier and more financing opportunities, so with the right team, you can grow your multifamily rental portfolio with ease. That team should include your attorney, bankers or lenders, multiple experienced contractors, and connect with a few good property management companies which can sometimes be life or death for a real estate investor. It's just very important that you have all of the pieces in place and you have people basically helping you run your multi family business.

Shannon:
Right when you began your real estate investing career, how important was it for you to establish a team to help you be successful?

Ram:
When I first got started, if I didn't have a team, I would have been much, much less profitable. The most important part of my team was my

mentor, and 2nd most important was my attorney, 3rd most important were my contractors. There are a lot of shady people that can try and take advantage of you, especially if you don't have the right team members in place. Your local investment community is the best place to look to build your team whether it's an attorney, or contractor. Anywhere I invest, I make sure to get out there and consistently network, and to see what company or which professional other investors are using, find out some of their resource if they're willing to share with me.

Shannon:
If someone was going to get started in real estate investing, we've talked about several things that are very important. What is the one thing that you would recommend they do first?

Ram:
I would definitely recommend them to get out there and start networking, get educated. There are lots of networking events that happen every week or every month. It depends on the location around the country. There are REIA's, there are super charged REIA's plus there are a lot of different local programs within your city which could be teaching how to fix windows, carpentry, trade shows, etc. Networking at these locations can help you possibly find partners, even a mentor to help you with your business, and you can connect with other local professionals, tradesman. Continuously, give out your cards and collect people's business cards, build your team or book of business, so that when you need a professional, you have multiple people to call at your fingertips.

Most local professionals know everybody else in town which can really help you when you are first starting out. It's also very important to get educated. If you don't have the right education, if you don't have the right foundation for your business, you're could be setting yourself up for failure. Beware of many of the solo guru investors who just started investing and they are also selling training. So, you have to make sure that you are setting yourself up tax wise, legal wise, knowledge wise, and be financially wise. Make sure that you have all of your ducks in a row before you 'jump' into that first real estate transaction.

Shannon:
What is a REIA?

Ram:
A REIA is a Real Estate Investing Association. There is a National Real Estate Investing Association, and you can look it up on the internet, search for your local chapter is. Every association is going to be different. There are some good ones, there may be some bad ones. Some REIA's sell nothing and may have general networking meetings. I do know of a few REIA's who use the education company where I am training, and I've seen some REIA's promote multiple tv gurus for financial gains. You have to just go out there, network, find a community that meets weekly, and if not, then monthly, experience it for yourself and make a decision on how you want to move forward with your business.

Shannon:
If you are starting with little or no money, or poor credit, what are some strategies that you can use to get into real estate?

Ram:
Use OPM or other people's money. One of the top methods that everybody wants to get into is wholesaling. You don't need a lot of money or credit to get started, but you have to be good at marketing, analyzing the market. Investors who have the knowledge can structure a joint venture deal, use other people's money to put together profitable transactions. Other strategies include investing in tax liens or tax deeds, acquiring property subject to (assuming someone's mortgage). Seller Financing and Lease options are also a great way to acquire a property with little to no money and give you time to raise money and capital to exercise the option, obtain financing to pay off your note, or sell the option to another buyer for a profit. With a good education and team, you can get creative and structure fix n flip or buy and hold transactions, or acquire property with little to no money of your own.

Shannon:
How do you minimize the risk of investing so that you can maximize your own success?

Ram:

It comes from a lot of market analysis, applying my education, discussing with colleagues, attorneys, my team, not rushing into any deal. It's very easy for mistakes to happen in real estate. For instance, you may estimate repair costs to be $30,000 to fix a house in a hurry, and once the work starts, you find there's more damage, and then it's going to cost you $60K or 90K, all because you rushed into the deal, didn't do an inspection. So, to maximize my success, I'm continuously working on my business, meeting my cpa's/agents/attorneys, go through my classes, and also just staying active with real estate networking meetings in the community helps me stay successful.

Shannon:

Sorry, I was on mute. Why do you think that people, what is the number one reason that you feel people fail at real estate?

Ram:

I feel it's a combination of factors, for instance not having the knowledge, then fear is a big one. Fear is a big killer of a lot of business. Another reason people fail is not maximizing their cash flow, whether it's through budgeting, meeting with their CPA, not budgeting for a project properly, just not having the cash needed can cause failure, and not having their whole team in place to help them. It's easy for bad things to happen in real estate, old pipes can break, people lose jobs all the time, people pass away, thieves can strip your home, things break at homes, sometimes you have to deal with tenants, you have to deal with toilets, extra taxes and insurance, and the list can go on, and some investors loose motivation, they give up easily. So, you have to take it slowly, understand the different strategies, understand what you are comfortable with doing as a real estate investor. Just like not everyone is good with a hammer, you need to find your niche, be able to wrap your head around all the pieces of your transaction, and move forward step by step.

Shannon:

What advice would you give to someone who is allowing fear to cripple them and hold them back?

Ram:

Well, it's like how do you handle any fear, take swimming. If somebody's scared of swimming or scared of the water, what do you do? You hold their hand and you go in with them. Same thing with real estate investing. If you're scared to go out there and make deals happen, find somebody who will help you out. Of course, there's a lot of shark investors out there, but there are also many nice real estate investors who will help you. I would also advise that someone to sit down with a real estate attorney or two, explain their business, their fears, their business plan. Once you find someone with a good reputation, and they agree to help you, you can show them, "Hey, I've got these resource, maybe you have to set up some sort of asset protection, or have some money set aside, get help looking at a potential deal but there are people out there that are willing to help you and they'll hold your hand, help alleviate those fears.

Shannon:

How does investing in commercial real estate expand your portfolio?

Ram:

Commercial real estate is great for investors who want to diversify their portfolio. There's a lot of uses for commercial real estate such as medical offices, industrial, retail, apartments, strip malls, warehouses, event or storage spaces, hotels, senior housing, student housing, and there are many more uses. In fact, we are in process of buying a commercial property right now through a lease option and that will be developed into senior housing and office space. So, there's lots of different uses that you can use commercial real estate for, and in many places around the country commercial is, right now, on sale.

Shannon:

Why do you think that is?

Ram:

I believe it also has to do with the economy, businesses fail, and then the commercial properties they are in also fail. When the economy gets stronger, then you have more residential and commercial development, leading to more commercial opportunities. The real estate market is a cyclic, whether it's residential or commercial real estate, there's always going to be ups and downs, if you compare the market to waves in an ocean, just don't get tossed around, know how to weather the storm, build a strong foundation.

Shannon:
What legacy do you want to leave?

Ram:
Well, besides my real estate empire of rentals and senior care facilities, I want my kids to continue my business of helping people achieve financial freedom and leave a positive impact on society. My parents have said to me multiple times that I was going to do something with medicine. After working in healthcare, it was obvious that families across the nation were suffering with their health because of their lack of wealth and the rat race struggle to make ends meet. This business has taught me the importance of being an entrepreneur, and my kids, who already work with me will be able to run their own multi million or even multi-billion-dollar business, and they can teach their kids, and grand kids to not only give back to society, but teach the masses different ways of building wealth with real estate, business ownership and spread what they have learned to new investors and entrepreneurs for generations to come.

Wojciech & Diana Przeczkowski

Wojciech Przeczkowski is an engineer, entrepreneur, life enthusiast, and small business owner. His hobbies include electronics, hiking, traveling with his wife, problem solving, and spending time with family and friends, as well as coming up with unique product and business ideas. Wojciech's entrepreneurial spirit was first ignited at a young age; and, before he was 30, he founded an app development company. Having graduated from the University of Illinois at Chicago with two engineering degrees, he quickly became a competitive leader in the industry with his diverse skillset. Publishing his Master's thesis in 2011 and being granted a patent in 2014, Wojciech become a senior level Electrical & Computer Engineer by 2016. Wojciech and his wife Diana started and incorporated their real estate business, Homegineering Inc., in 2016 and acquired a fix and flip rehab project with an ARV of almost half a million dollars.

Diana graduated from The Illinois Institute of Art—Chicago, with a degree in Interior Design. Her hard work, unique design talents, and clever work ethic quickly took her from a facilities planner to a project manager. Having acquired her Illinois Real Estate Broker's license in 2016, she's jumped into the real estate market as a broker, interior designer, and an investor. She's since earned multiple awards for highest grossing listing agent and most listings in a month. Diana has grown Homegineering Inc's team of contractors and investors. She's extremely dedicated to building and expanding her business. The couple enjoy traveling together and are always looking for their next project. They overcome challenges together and make time for family, friends, and faith.

Contact info:

Wojciech Przeczkowski

     Website: www.homegineering.com

     Email: wojo@homegineering.com

Diana Przeczkowski

     Website: www.yourchicagolandrealtor.com

     Email: diana@yourchicagolandrealtor.com

       diana@homegineering.com

Shannon:

What inspired you to get into real estate?

Wojciech:

The opportunity to live the American dream. The opportunity to build and grow a small business using creative strategies while taking advantage of business tax benefits. Real estate investing is about becoming educated and connecting with people. This is one of the few businesses where you save people's lives and their livelihoods. Imagine the satisfaction you feel when you have the ability to save people's properties from bank or court seizure, for example, by sharing your investor knowhow with people who need it most. I think that's very rewarding.

Shannon:

How about you, Diana?

Diana:

I come from a little bit different background than my husband, but I was always interested in architecture, interior design, and in my opinion real estate is the extension of that. I always wanted to help people create their environments, preserve their livelihoods, and help to live their lives a little better. Real estate allows me to extend my arm and help people in need, and at the same time create the life I always imagined.

Shannon:

When you began your real estate investing career, how important was it for you to establish a team to help you be successful?

Wojciech:

At first, I never really thought anything of that topic. I just figured I was going to do all this by myself. I learned very quickly that in addition to having knowledge in real estate investing, which doesn't happen overnight, it was critical to expand my network in order to be successful. I'm able to reach out to people throughout the country and get answers to my questions. It's important to get out of your comfort zone and talk with people openly. If you think about it, your net worth is proportional to your network.

Shannon:

What would you say is the number one mistake an individual makes when buying their first investment property?

Diana:

Not doing the numbers right or not having knowledge how to analyze a deal properly I would say is the number one mistake. Another mistake of rookie investors is to get into deals with emotion as opposed to with intellect.

Shannon:

Expand on that for me, Diana.

Diana:

For example, it would be a huge mistake to get into a deal in real estate not doing proper comparables, not carefully calculating the after repair value or ARV, and basically just thinking or hoping that you are going to make money on this particular property. That's the biggest mistake that people make.

Shannon:

You also touched on emotion...

Diana:

Yes, I did.

Shannon:

What do you mean by that?

Diana:

As a woman, I was more inclined to be interested in a property based on my emotions. It was because I personally liked the kitchens or the bathrooms or because of my preference of use of space. As one starts

investing in real estate and getting into buying investment properties, they cannot make decisions using emotions. You need to have
done all of your calculations before going into a deal to make sure
you will get a desirable return on your investment. If the numbers
don't make sense, don't become attached trying to massage some
return you will never get.

Shannon:
What is one of the top real estate strategies that you have learned?

Wojciech:
Creatively financing your deals. There are many financing methods
beyond going to the bank for a loan. There are also creative ways of
finding and acquiring properties. Did you know there are trillions of
dollars in the nation's retirement accounts such as 401ks and IRAs
that could be yielding much higher rates of return if they invested in
real estate rather than stocks, bonds, or mutual funds?

Shannon:
*If you're starting with little or no money, how do you use any of those
strategies?*

Wojciech:
A real estate investor, being a business owner, is also a problem
solver. Creatively and responsibly you figure out solutions. You grow
and reach out to people who you know: your network, your friends
and family, your warm market. That opens up the door for private
money funding and being able to grow your business.

Shannon:
*How does learning multiple investing strategies protect and accelerate
your investing success?*

Wojciech:
Although I believe it's important to have multiple strategies, in the
beginning you should master one. Learning and becoming proficient

at one investment strategy will give you the confidence, financing, and team to help you with moving into the next. Having multiple strategies diversifies your portfolio and your assets. You can offer value to people with your knowledge in multiple investment strategies. That helps grow your network and your business, which contributes to your success.

Shannon:

Do you feel that real estate investing success is dependent on a strong economy?

Diana:

Not necessarily. If you're an educated real estate investor, economy does not make any difference. The market might be strong now, but even after it crashes, there will be plenty of opportunities out there. In a strong market, investors are able deal with properties all over the spectrum. On the other hand, when the economy gets worse, there are more opportunities to work creatively and find properties beyond just using MLS for example. In a bad economy investors have an opportunity to offer more value to other people and at the same time make positive cash flow. So to answer your question, I don't think real estate investing success is dependent on a strong economy. You can make a lot of money using various investment strategies that work for different markets and economic conditions.

Wojciech:

May I add to that? There are many things in the economy, for example in our particular county in the state of Illinois we just got our property taxes increased. That indirectly affects people buying homes. The economy does have effects, but when you look at it in general, there are many niches in real estate investing where if the market goes up or down, you're still protected and making money.

Shannon:

What's a good niche to go into in a weak economy?

Diana:

I would say rentals, or buy and hold properties. When people cannot afford to buy a home in the weak economy, they still need a place to live. This niche offers positive cash flow from month to month for the investor and more importantly a home for someone.

Shannon:

What is a good investment strategy to get into in a strong economy?

Wojciech:

In a strong economy, when property values are increasing, getting involved with fix and flips is a good investment strategy. You get in and get out and make a profit. You splash on some new paint, replace the carpet or refinish the floors, update the kitchen, update the bathrooms, and flip it. In a strong economy, the comparable properties in the area should be increasing in value along with yours. So even if you do minor work, your ARV will most likely come out higher than you originally thought.

Shannon:

What is cash flow? Why is it important?

Wojciech:

Cash flow is regularly still being paid while relaxing on vacation! Rentals produce cash flow from the regular rents they generate. It's important for a real estate investor to acquire rentals or properties that cash flow. This cash flow can then be used to fund fix and flip projects, for example. If your long-term goal is to leave your full-time job and focus your efforts on running a business, you'll need to supplement your income with incoming cash flow from your projects. Acquiring cash flow assets will help replace your income that you may only be getting from a full-time job at the moment and produce residual income down the line.

Shannon:

What's one of the things that you can do to make sure that you don't go over budget?

Wojciech:

You do careful deal analysis. You do careful calculations. You compare enough deals to become comfortable and accurate when analyzing deals. It's important to compare deals on a regular basis to stay sharp. When you're in a deal, you keep track of all your planned expenses, progress, and unexpected expenses. You'd be surprised how easy it is to underestimate the true cost of repairs. If you don't know how much a kitchen or bathroom costs, how can you confidently stick to your budget? Remember, you're a real estate investor and not a contractor. Regular deal analysis, whether you'll be getting into that deal or not, helps develop an accurate budget for when the right deal does come along.

Make sure you get quotes from multiple contractors. Don't always assume that your house is going to sell with an ARV of the high comparable in the community because sometimes that might not be the case, especially with changing market conditions. Keep in mind that there will surely be many unexpected expenses and you need to plan for those as well.

Shannon:

How does real estate allow you to earn passive, and massive, income?

Wojciech:

Passive income would be income from a cash flowing asset such as a rental or multi-unit property. Even a fix and flip project can be converted into a cash flowing rental. Once you get a few of those up and running, have reliable tenants (not professional tenants, as they call them), then you have regular income coming in. All you really need to do is just manage your cash flowing properties, or if you have too many to manage efficiently, hire a management company. If you have all of this set up you can easily scale this to two, three, or more multi-family units each generating passive income. Over time this will generate massive income.

When planning to generate massive income, realize that it's not going to happen overnight. It's not going to make you an instant millionaire. These things, these assets, these systems take time to implement and scale. Most importantly, by investing in yourself, there's what's called a compound effect that happens. One good thing generates another good thing, and those two outcomes motivate further effects and outcomes, and eventually you have the snowball effect. Ask yourself this question: Would you take $5 million upfront or a penny doubled every day over 30 days? Most people would be quick to grab that $5 million because we all like instant gratification. Well, if you look at it, on day 30 that penny has grown to over $5.3 million dollars due to the compounding effect law. You need to apply this mindset when starting to earn passive income, providing value to the community and others, and the byproduct will naturally be massive income. Start slow and implement systems that work. Your systems can then be scaled over time and before you know it you'll have multiple cash flowing assets generating massive income.

Shannon:
Diana, if someone wanted to get started into real estate, what would you recommend they do first?

Diana:
I would recommend you get educated first, and then take action. When you have enough knowledge, go ahead and search and analyze deals, and when the numbers make sense, close the deal and just dive into it because that way you'll learn the most. You learn by taking action. Even if you get burned at first, or along the way, don't stop. At some point you will get seasoned enough to be a master at investing. If something doesn't go the way you want it, at least you know you will have the experience for your next deals. Real estate is constantly evolving and there are many factors which contribute to being successful at it.

Shannon:
What advice would you give to someone who is afraid to start, so they're allowing fear to hold them back?

Wojciech:
I would draw them a timeline of their life and explain to them that the longer they wait or keep putting off their dreams and aspirations, the

longer that time can never be gotten back. We humans have approximately 29,200 days in an average 80-year lifespan. That's about 29,200 wake ups and opportunities to do something great with our lives. Do something, anything, and if you're telling yourself that you'll start tomorrow, you're just coming up with an excuse for today! When time is up and you're departing from this world, do you think you'll regret doing the things you did, or regret not doing the things you could've done? I think we all might know the answer to that question.

Wojciech:
Also, be wary of the criticisms from your friends and family. Don't let anyone convince you that something is too hard or impossible or that you're crazy for trying. Chances are, they are probably not an expert in whatever it is they are trying to talk you out of, so why should their opinions influence what you want to do? Seek advice from experts, find a mentor, ask questions, and don't be afraid to try new things. Success is basically the sum of all your failures. You will fail along the way, but you'll learn from those failures and continue trying. Eventually having gone through many iterations and many failures you will succeed in whatever it is that you are pursuing.

Diana:
Exactly. Don't take to heart some of the things other people will say along your entrepreneurial journey. You might seem crazy to someone who doesn't have an entrepreneurial mindset. Educate these people or stir up an interesting topic and have them ask questions which will help them realize certain things. Go on websites, read articles, learn from other real estate investors, get a mentor, just learn, learn, learn, and then once you know enough, get out there and just do it. Take action.

Shannon:
In your business, how do you help others learn more about real estate investing?

Wojciech:
By example. Having something to show for is good. It builds a lot of

credibility. In the beginning, we really didn't have anything to show for, not even an incorporated business. We were reading books, watching videos, and meeting likeminded people, but until we incorporated our business and got into our first deal and started talking about it, people started asking questions and we were able to provide good answers. People are hesitant to start their own businesses and righteously so, it's not easy. People like to hear your story, about your challenges, and how you overcame them. A good story goes a long way. Everything is difficult before it is easy.

Shannon:

What specifically do you do? How do you teach them, so do you have networking events? Do you have dinners? Do you have them come walk a job with you? How do you help others learn more about real estate?

Wojciech:

We hold cash recovery parties; we've had many open houses and invited friends and family. Having a YouTube channel helps as well as having many websites. Hosting property tours helps because you can explain to people exactly what you did and have lots to show for. Plus, you meet new people and, remember, your net worth is proportional to your network. Keep your network growing because it will help you grow as a real estate investor.

Inviting people to a property tour or an open house of a real estate project you're working on really helps. The power of the internet and social media also provides many outlets to reach out to people. Organizing and hosting Meetups is very useful. You can teach people using the video streaming features of Facebook. You can create your YouTube channel and upload regular weekly videos. Additionally, hosting a party with pizza or whatever food you prefer, with no alcohol, and inviting your friends and family helps as well. You can write off the event food from your taxable income, eat, and enlighten people. At that pizza party you can play them a few educational videos explaining to them some really cool real estate concepts and strategies as well as tax saving strategies by having a small business. It's priceless to see people's reactions when they find their eureka moments during those parties.

I noticed an interesting thing happens to your friends and family when you leave the pack. Most people go about their days in a typical fashion. People don't like change or deviation. When your friends and family see you leave their pack because you've started a business, are meeting successful people, flipping houses, and talking your entrepreneurial babble, some start to feel left out. At the very least they begin to ask questions and they become interested in your new life. They talk and explain to their friends that they learned something new and now indirectly their friends are interested in what you do and they begin asking questions. It's quite interesting to see this process unfold.

Diana:

When we acquired our first property and started working on it, our friends, which was very strange to me, were coming out to the property un-announced just to look at it. This is basically how we began talking to them and told them about real estate investing and what we were doing. I mean, it was to the point that they were coming with their families, with their parents, which was very cool to see.

Shannon:

All right. Diana, how has real estate investing changed your life?

Diana:

Oh, my goodness. First, I'm much more open to conversations with other people than I was before. Second, it seems to be a total mind transformation to me. I see myself being free of working for someone else's success; instead I'm building my own empire. I did my real estate license last year to help our business grow, and now I'm a licensed real estate agent in Illinois which helps us with finding deals. I'm already looking into expanding nationally. I regularly look and analyze properties now with a keener eye, it's what I love to do. I don't consider being a real estate investor as having another job, it's become part of my life. I become excited when driving around and seeing properties for sale. Becoming a partner in a brokerage firm has given me the confidence and skillset I need to do well in this business. I cannot wait for what the future holds.

Wojciech:

Plus keeping that sales commission in the family is a good move if you're serious about being a real estate investor. I'm very proud of Diana getting her real estate license and being part of our real estate investing business. I can focus on growing the business and she can focus on finding and selling deals. We complement each other very well in my opinion.

Diana:

That is true. Yet, it turned my life upside down. I'm at the point right now where I am able to quit my full time job, just to do real estate full time. That's a liberating feeling!

Shannon:

What does that mean to you?

Diana:

It means freedom to me. I won't have to wake up at five o'clock in the morning every day and go to someone else's office to work for their success. I won't have to waste an hour and half driving each way, instead I can be working on getting more investment properties or more deals. I will be able to do what I absolutely love, which is helping others get out of uncomfortable living situations. So, it means freedom to me. It means financial freedom and time freedom. It is absolutely rewarding to be able to do whatever I want with my life.

Shannon:

Wojciech, how has real estate changed your life?

Wojciech:

It's allowed me to realize that there are alternatives to the whole nine to five; well nowadays it's more like eight to six, typical full-time job, with only ten vacation days per year. We live in one of the most promising countries in the world for the pursuit of happiness and success. It's allowed me to realize that I have the opportunity to work directly on my own success, rather than for somebody else's success.

Starting your own business is really a quite simple concept, but it's not easy. Simple and easy are two different things. It's also turned my life upside down because I think every entrepreneur is a little bit crazy, but they need to be because you have to cross that fear threshold and keep pushing. Where others might stop or quit, having that entrepreneurial craziness is what keeps you pushing through.

It's also allowed me to take risks. It's allowed me to get into responsible debt. I mean, you know, people would think being half a million dollars in debt is a bad thing. Well, not really, if you're educated and you've done your numbers, then you can use debt to earn profits. It's made me realize that starting your own business in America, whether it is real estate or some other small business, is possible if you just turn off that season rerun of your TV show and take action each and every day. Taking small action regularly and habitually generates positive outcomes in your life.

Shannon:
Diana, Wojciech just told us all that he's a little crazy? Are you also a little crazy, or do you consider yourself more of the numbers and the fact checking person of this team?

Wojciech:
She's nuts.

Diana:
I think I'm more nuts than Wojciech is.

Shannon:
Okay. Perfect. You are also a little crazy. Perfect.

Diana:
Oh yes. Absolutely

Shannon:
What is the legacy that you want to leave behind? Why do you do what you do?

Wojciech:

People have different whys and reasons for the things they pursue. Sometimes we do things because we want to better ourselves. Sometimes we want to become stronger after a tragedy happens. It's important to find your why because it gives your life and ambitions a purpose. It's important to overlook the profits and concentrate on the why in the beginning. The profits will be byproducts of your why.

When I graduated from the University of Illinois with a BS in Computer Engineering and a MS in Electrical and Computer Engineering, I began working full time just to be laid off multiple times from multiple companies. Nine months into my first job, the company got bought out by another company and everyone was laid off. No big deal I thought, I found another job at a major US defense contractor just to be laid off after two years due to budget cuts and the recession. I began asking myself, wait a minute, I went to college, got these fancy engineering degrees, and this is how it's going to work until I retire in my 60s?! I then worked for another company where I knew I was underpaid for the work that I did. Our salaries were even cut by 10 percent for an entire year. Eventually, the company got bought out by a larger company, upper management got golden parachutes, and they explained to me that my salary would remain the same. They even gave me a fancy title to help justify not increasing my salary. That was my tipping point. At that point, an entrepreneur with a will to never give up was born. I thought to myself, this is not how I want to live anymore. I need to work for myself and not for anyone else. A good mentor of mine, Bob, once told me that your true worth is so much more than just a salary, that someone else dictates for that particular position.

Ever since we started our real estate investing business with my wife, there have been many challenges. Just recently in 2017, my younger brother and only sibling passed away. This was a huge shock to me and changed my perspective on life. He helped me so much on the project. I told him it was difficult for me to see the final project be done and he kept telling me that it's going to happen and when it does it will be beautiful and that I will be proud to see it and all the hard work we put into it. I saw how beautiful it turned out, unfortunately he didn't get that chance. My brother and his memory are part of my 'why' for doing anything. A friend and fellow real estate investor once told me, "you owe it to your brother to live your life not just for you or your wife, but in honor of him as well."

Some people say they 'want to kill time,' others live for the weekend. Well, you might not live until next weekend because that's just how life works. Living life as if it would be my last day gives me my drive, gives me power and motivation to do what I do. It's not until we're at our weakest moments where we come up with our greatest ideas, or greatest decisions, but sometimes we have to be placed in those moments to grow. Finally, my why is my family, my wife, my time remaining on this earth. Not having to be told how much you're worth by a salary number because I know I'm worth way more than that as a human being.

Diana:

My why is my family, my parents, brother, sisters, my nieces and nephews, my entire life moving forward. These people are the reasons I do what I do. Another reason why is to show other people that anything you put your mind and heart into is possible. It doesn't matter if someone doesn't believe in you, you have to believe in yourself, always. Nothing is too hard to achieve, and I want to show others that's absolutely true.

I came to the U.S. as a 20-year-old right after finishing high school with $20 in my pocket and no knowledge of the English language. I came to the U.S. with huge aspirations of being successful and to achieve higher education in music performance playing cello. After a few months, I decided to switch gears and study interior design, since I was always passionate about design and architecture. Everyone I knew was telling me I would not be able to thrive as a musician and my life would be quite miserable. I didn't know any better then, but now I know I could be thriving in anything I take on. After graduating from the Art Institute of Chicago, I started working as an interior designer, then a store planner, facilities planner, and now a project manager. None of these jobs or titles gave me complete feelings of self-fulfillment. I always wanted to help people and not just be a part of a corporation making profits for itself and not caring more about its employees. I always wanted others to lead better and more fulfilled lives. My mantra is to help people achieve happiness through the environments they live in.

I'd like to leave a lasting legacy for my family's generations—just so they don't have to struggle to make ends meet. So they don't have to wonder where the next paycheck is going to come from and how they are going to be able to pay their bills. So they don't struggle through life but rather thrive and be happy. So that the future generations will be able to take on whatever they want—even if it's music performance or the arts.

Shelley Sims

Shelley has the quintessential entrepreneurial spirit. Throughout the creation of eight businesses, she has always had a fond place in her heart for transformation, whether it be through spiritual studies, or event planning, or property remodeling. She is active and passionate about creating a better life for herself and those around her. She utilizes her constant desire to learn and educate herself to share and empower others to improve too. She is a visionary and utilizes her organization and management skills to create those visions in the physical world. Her determination keeps her moving through any barriers. She is the CEO of Thrive Inc., a real estate Investing company in Colorado that's main focus is on fixing and flipping and brokering seller financed notes.

Contact Info:
Shelley@thriveincrealestate.com
970.688.0886
www.thriveincrealestate.com

Shannon:

What inspired you to get into real estate investing?

Shelley:

I grew up around real estate my entire life. My dad was an agent/ investor/developer, my stepdad was an agent/developer, my grandfather and my uncle both owned Moore and Company, a locally owned and managed real estate brokerage, and they loved developing land. It all started with my great-grandfather on my mother's side. He started Moore & Company in Loveland, Colorado, back in the early 1900s. In fact, he was the oldest living active real estate agent in Colorado when he passed away at the age of 96. He had sold his last house the day before. It is easy to say real estate is in my blood. Everywhere we went growing up, we were constantly looking at either a condo, a home, or a shopping mall or going all around to look at raw land that somebody wanted to develop. I was raised to believe real estate was the "only way" to make money. As I got older, I had tried selling and being a real estate agent and working in the relocation division of our family's company. I wasn't very good working for anyone else as an employee, and I continued my search for my place in the world. I was too young, I think, at the time. As time went on, I learned that I had the influence of fashion in my life from my mother's love. I became a perfect combination of a real estate dad and fashion mom. I created my own business doing interior design.

Shannon:

Plays well into investing, doesn't it?

Shelley:

It definitely does because what ended up happening is I got a chance to do a lot of updating and beautifying of properties for my clients. I have a lot of experience managing projects, and my favorite kinds of projects are the ones where clients lived outside of the state, and I got to run the crew, be the general contractor, be the interior designer, even once in a while going in and doing the last-minute dusting. I did everything to make sure that the properties were beautiful for the clients, so they could just come and enjoy the Colorado mountains. As I continued to think, "Wow, where do I want to go? What do I want to do?" I looked back to my life of when I was the happiest. I was always the happiest in the middle of these transformation projects with these properties.

Shannon:
Basically, you just woke up one morning and you thought, "This is where I was happiest. I'm going to start doing this," or did you run into someone who you then thought, "Oh my gosh, this is it. Here's how I get it."

Shelley:
It of course, is not that simple, but the long story short is that I had a spiritual teacher that suggested I buy a home. Her suggestion opened up an entire larger picture point of view that I had never imagined before. And before I knew it, step by step, I was creating a new fantastic life for myself. I loved being at the closing table on both the buying and selling side. Then I worked with a friend in Boulder who was offering me a property to rent to do as a fix and flip. That was of course against all rules in anyone's mind to rent a property and start flipping it before I owned it. I have a bit of rebellion in me, and although I had no idea how to do that, and was quite fearful, I knew I could. I remember the fear I had the first day I stepped into Sutherlands Lumber in Boulder. I didn't know anything about being a contractor or doing any of those things, but I worked up my courage, and ever since that day of moving through those fears, I have loved the entire remodeling process. Fast forward many years, and I had been managing many projects and always saying to myself, "I would really love to get into fixing and flipping and real estate investing, if I knew how to look at the deals and raise the money, and if I had money behind me, I would just do that all day long." It was quite a process from that one day going into the lumber yard versus where I am right now. I am supercharging my investing career, and I knew I needed a lot more training and education so that I wasn't diving blindly into a situation where I could get myself in trouble.

Shannon:

How long ago was that when rented you a property to fix?

Shelley:

That was back in 1999.

Shannon:

Take that experience and put it in today. Let's say you met someone today who said, "Sure, I want rent you this property that you can fix and flip." What would you say? What would you do the same? What would you do differently?

Shelley:

What I would do the same is I would continue stepping through all of my fears and taking the steps, trusting and knowing and following my intuition that I could do it. What I would do differently is I would structure the deal differently. I would make some different decisions on finish materials. Maybe minor details on finish sizes and dimensions and different things. Most importantly, what I would do is I would structure the deal differently, so that I wasn't taking such a risk as I did back then.

Shannon:

What would that look like today, so that you could protect yourself?

Shelley:

It would look like something rather than the rental process; it would look something like a seller finance ownership process or a lease option agreement. Something where I have official control and not just relying on universal love and blind trust.

Shannon:

Not just a handshake and a prayer?

Shelley:

Exactly. I laugh at myself because it's one of the most beautiful parts about me, and it's also one of the more challenging aspects about me.

Shannon:

What is that? Our strengths and our weaknesses are the exact same thing.

Shelley:

Exactly.

Shannon:

Our weaknesses are our strengths, overused.

Shelley:

Exactly. Faith and trust ...

Shannon:

Yes, exactly.

Shelley:

Perfect.

Shannon:

Now you are having your real estate investing career rejuvenated?

Shelley:

Yes!

Shannon:

I'm guessing that you have a mentor, someone that you look up to?

Shelley:

Yes. I'm very lucky because I have many mentors. I would say specifically there are 10 people that I know I can dial on the phone and ask questions to at any moment. I'm super grateful for that because compared to that situation in the previous time, I had one person. With hindsight, it wasn't any one of my family members and it wasn't the rich dad or the rich uncle, it was someone else who was doing her best to try to make it and get by. I have come full circle now; I have gathered a nice team of people on which to rely and ask questions and be inspired by.

Shannon:

Tell me about a time when one of those mentors, one or more in your real estate investing, helped you to navigate a potential pitfall.

Shelley:

Just recently, I was the middle of working with a homeowner who was in foreclosure, and we were discussing how we could structure a contract to help her and to help ourselves as investors. One of the great comments that my mentor said to me was something very off-the-cuff of, "What makes you think she's going be able to make a rent payment to you, when she's not making her mortgage payment now?" It seemed like such a very basic understanding or point of view, but because I was getting in the middle of it and getting excited by the process and getting excited by the potential outcome, I had become blindsided. Just that one little question gave me the detachment and the perspective to say, «Yeah, you better think twice about this, Shelley.» I am structuring something differently because of that insight.

I love those kinds of moments where my awareness expands because of the other person's experience and expertise. I love when I am asked a question and my entire perspective changes. It helps me see from the larger point of view.

Shannon:

I think people who process like you, and I process very similarly to you, get very excited about things and I think, just because they haven't done it before doesn't mean that they wouldn't or couldn't.

Shelley:

Yes. That's very true.

Shannon:

You know, sometimes I need a reality check, too. That being said ...

Shelley:

Yes, both are true. Because that comment isn't going stop me from proceeding, it's just going to allow me to be smarter in how I structure my offer.

Shannon:

Got it.

Shelley:

You're right. I do have that bigger view picture point of view that just because it hasn't happened before doesn't mean It can't, and that positive perspective of the glass being half full... just because she hasn't been able to yet, maybe she can. I always have that more positive point of view thought, and the wisdom of experience and the other mentor's point of view does make me be smarter in my actions.

Shannon:

Here's a question because you seem pretty fearless to me. What advice would you give someone who is allowing fear to hold them back from starting their real estate investing career?

Shelley:

For years and years I've always said to myself, and I don't remember who I heard this from, "Feel the fear, and do it anyway." At times I would really shy away from that thing that I feared. But now I use the fear to propel me. I'm really liking now to just lean into it, so that it's not the jumping off the bridge, jumping into the fear, fearlessly making stupid decisions, not knowing what I am doing. It's more of a gentle leaning in with knowledge and experience and using the wisdom that I have, but letting the fear guide me and direct me to where I need to go. In fact, I use it to help guide me towards the next steps.

Shannon:

On the contrary side, if you met someone who was completely fearless and just jumping in, both feet, what advice would you give them?

Shelley:

I might suggest that they reel it in a little bit and maybe go more slowly, depending on the situation. If they're jumping in and then creating a lot of havoc and chaos in their life, I would say maybe they need to stop and think first before they jump.

Shannon:

Someone comes to you and says, "I'm ready. I am ready, I want to start my real estate investing career." What's the first piece of advice you would give them? What should they do first?

Shelley:

They should find knowledgeable, smart, successful, people to learn from.

Shannon:

You make that sound really easy. How do they do that?

Shelley:

I do make that sound easy because there are tons of people out there teaching real estate investing. There are events happening every month with someone coming to town offering education. I was definitely looking for something new and different in my life. I knew it was possible to be living a different life than what I was living. I knew my design business had been up and down, and I was tired of it being up and down. I wanted to even out the extremes and be more in the middle. I was looking and open and in a lot of ways very desperate for something great to happen. That's how I found Renatus; I was looking on craigslist and I saw the ad that said, "Real estate investor seeks trainee." I was attracted to that because I knew I didn't know how to do it very well. I knew I had been exposed to it, I knew real estate was a very important, great, wonderful, strong, avenue that I would love to be in, and I didn't know how to do it, to create a system and generate a lot of money. If I could learn how to do it, the trainee part, then I would be able to take some of those same risks that I took in the past without the knowledge and create a better life for myself. I could save myself money, time, heartache, by knowing how to do it better than I did back then. My advice to anyone else wanting to do real estate investing is to get educated from people who are experts and are already successful doing investing. Don't waste your time flailing here and there and going all over YouTube and getting a bunch of free education that you don›t even know if those people are successful at doing what they›re preaching.

Shannon:

That's awesome advice. What is your favorite strategy? You talked about fix and flip. Do you like doing fix and flips? Are you looking to maybe build your portfolio with buy and holds? Are you looking to do multi-family dwellings? What is your avenue? What do you want to do? What are you doing?

Shelley:

I am currently analyzing properties for fixing and flipping because I know that's one of my strengths, and I know that I can do that easily. I also think they take a lot of time, and I want to find some easier ways to make money. My newest endeavor is brokering seller-financed notes. I see huge potential for still being able to help people get the funds that they need, get the investors to have the returns that they want, being the middleman, and doing it with less heavy lifting, so I would like to say, as it would take for a fix and flip. I have also dreams of creating multi-family dwellings and holding them for passive income. I have visions of apartments buildings with different travel themes. I will create an Asia building using colors and architectural aspects in the design elements. And a building that is influenced by France or Spain or Argentina or something fun like that. I envision myself owning lots of apartment buildings with different destination names. It's a nice combination of the design creativity, real estate, and my love of travel.

Shannon:

I love how creative you are with your thoughts, with your properties, with your vision. Do you think that creativity is going to come in handy when you are looking to acquire property?

Shelley:

Yes. I think that creativity is going to come in handy during the process of structuring the many options for a homeowner. Let's say that I find a pre-foreclosure woman who's about to go to auction in two weeks, and she doesn't have any options herself, but through my creative knowledge and experience and education, I am able to offer one, two, three different scenarios that may be beneficial for her, for me, for everyone involved. My goal in all of the endeavors that I'm doing is to create positive situations for everyone involved. I am not that person that just goes and takes advantage of people. I like to help myself and help other people help other people, and so on.

Shannon:

I hear that in real estate a lot of real estate investors say win-win. I'll tell you I don't come from a real estate background, I come from just business. In business it's kind of a running joke that there's never a win-win. There's always a winner and a loser. Explain to me how do you create a win-win?

Shelley:

It takes a lot of questions, and it takes a lot of thorough consideration of what all the parties need. What do I need, what do the investors need? I take into account a number of different factors. Let's just compare that to what it's like when I'm doing a fix and flip. There's a number of different factors that come into play. What kind of tile am I going to use, what kind of paint am I using, what's the layout of the room that's going to be best for that property if I need to rearrange the kitchen? Who is the perfect person that will live here and what do they need? To compare investing to design, it is like the creating the floor plan or the flow of energy through the room. With every deal, there's a flow of energy through the deal.

It comes from being the point person in the middle of the spoke. I think of myself as the person in the middle of the spoke, and I know the information of the owner, and their bank, and their financial situation, and I know the investor, and their situation, and their required return. I know my investor identity, so I know what I want to be making on my return and the amount of time or effort that I do or don't have to spend on it. I'm taking all of the big picture information into consideration and then structuring something accordingly.

Shannon:

Love it. Basically, everybody leaves feeling good. Does everybody leave making money?

Shelley:

In my world, yes. Everybody leaves with a good feeling that they got what they needed from the situation.

Shannon:

You touched a little bit about how right now you are working on brokering seller-financed notes. Explain to me what that means?

Shelley:

A seller-financed note is a promissory note that is held by a previous homeowner, written by the new buyer. A homeowner has a home, they want to sell it, the new person buying may not be able to qualify for conventional mortgage for whatever reason. They might not have the kind of income, they might not have the credit score. The new buyer then relies on the seller to carry the note for them. The seller basically becomes the bank for that new buyer. There's an entire marketplace to sell that note and receive cash at a discount. It is even possible to sell partial payments on a note and receive some cash.

Let's say it's a $100,000 note. They could buy the full note at a discounted rate, whatever that might be, based on the investor's return that they're wanting to get, and/or they could sell partial payments. They might be able to sell just the next 10 payments. Let's say the seller has a daughter that's getting married, and they need some extra cash to help pay for the wedding, and they don't have that just sitting around in their savings account, but they have this promissory note from the house that they sold. They could go sell the next 10 payments, get the money to be able to pay for the daughter's wedding, and still have the rest of the balance of the balloon of that mortgage due towards them later on.

It is a fantastic investing strategy that benefits all involved.

Shannon:

It sounds so risky to me. When you're speaking to someone who's not as educated, how do you make sure that they understand their risks and that way not only you are protected but so are they?

Shelley:

People that invest in notes are pretty experienced or very experienced. They know what their risk tolerance is, and they adjust their percentage or yield of return according to their risk tolerance. The people that need the most education in this particular transaction are the people who are the noteholders. Because many of them are less experienced.

My job in these situations is to educate and inform. I think of it as a position of coaching noteholders, homeowners, how to make wise financial decisions with the assets they currently own.

Shannon:

Put it for me into layman's terms. Your noteholder, your previous home-owner, why would they do a seller finance? Doesn't that prevent them from being able to use another loan to purchase another home?

Shelley:

It completely depends on their financial situation, but they would do it because they want to make additional income by charging the interest. Rather than Wells-Fargo coming in and loaning the new buyer money and the seller receiving the $100,000 for the house that they sold, they might be able to sell the house for $110,000 plus the interest of maybe 9 percent, so the seller would be benefiting by making more money in the end.

Shannon:

It seems like it's a longer-term investment. Is that a correct statement?

Shelley:

Yes, it is. If there was another type of financing, then the seller is out of it, they're done, they don't have anything to do with it ever again. If they are the bank there is collecting the payments and some logistics to take care of. And they can earn money on the interest. It just depends on their desired goals and financial situation of the seller.

Shannon:

Got it. Is real estate investing success dependent on a strong economy?

Shelley:

No. Not if you're experienced in multiple strategies. If you only have one strategy as an investor and you can only do this one type of transaction, then yes, you will be affected by the ups and downs. If you learn numerous strategies, and you have different ways to implement particular strategies at different time frames depending on what the market is doing, then you can weather the storm.

Shannon:

What is one strategy that you can use to acquire a home for doing a fix and flip in a strong economy?

Shelley:

Probate is a good strategy almost any time. This is the case where a homeowner has passed away, and the heirs have inherited a property that they don't know what to do with, or are fighting over. As an investor, helping them sell the property allows them to distribute the funds and finish out the inheritance. That's a good strategy, anytime.

Shannon:

Explain to me one strategy for acquiring real estate in a weak economy. The housing bubble just burst again. What do you do? How do you acquire properties, and how do you make money? How do you not lose your shirt in real estate when the housing bubble just burst?

Shelley:

That's where knowing the foreclosure process is important. There are many steps in the process before a property goes to auction and is officially foreclosed on. Pre-foreclosure is a very nice way to help people so that they don't have to experience foreclosure on their record and the shame, and the upset, and having to be evicted from their home.

Shannon:

This is a long-term thing for you. This is your last career it sounds like?

Shelley:

Yes!

Shannon:

Do you see yourself being ready when our economy does turn again, and how do you see yourself wanting to work in that pre-foreclosure market?

Shelley:

YES! I am ready because of the education and the mentors that I have surrounded myself with. I continue to stay on the cutting edge of what is happening in the marketplace, and I have numerous creative abilities to help people with their real estate problems. For a homeowner who has received a letter that the foreclosure process has begun, I would suggest three possible solutions.

First, I sit down with them and get to know them by asking many questions, so I can find out more about their unique situation and what they really need. I help them to take action.

The first step is to have them contact their bank to find out exactly all the details and amounts of what is owed to become current. Often the banks will work with them to remedy the situation. This is an important part of helping the homeowner. One of the largest challenges is getting them to help face the situation. The upset and shame and emotions that come along with not being able to make your bills keeps a person from acting at all, and that is the very worst thing to do. Sometimes they simply need a bit of encouragement.

The second way that I help people in foreclosure is to make an offer to buy their home at a set price that we agree upon. Something that works for them and me as the investor.

The third way to structure a transaction could be to keep their financing in place, and allow me as the investor to buy the property subject to the existing loan. I would create an agreement to repair the home and then sell it at a profit and share the proceeds with the homeowner. This is a wonderful way for me to access a property with very little money into it and allows the homeowner an opportunity to make money in a way they may not know how to do. It is this type of thinking outside the box that really gets fun.

Shannon:
You have a good strong team of people. You've already talked about how you have mentors. You are in Colorado. The housing market is strong, and houses are expensive there. Is that frightening to you to invest in real estate at such high dollar amounts, as opposed to areas such as Ohio or Texas where you can literally buy two-for-one homes?

Shelley:
No, it's not frightening at all.

Shannon:
Why?

Shelley:
I like to invest in what I know. I am a native of Colorado, and I feel comfortable with Colorado. With the training and education, I am able to find off-market properties at a discount, no matter what the market is doing. Even in the difficult times, there are areas in Colorado that have held their value, so I am not worried about investing in a high market. I am just more selective. I'd much rather invest in what I know than go venture into areas that I am unfamiliar with.

Shannon:
What kind of legacy do you want to leave behind?

Shelley:
I would like to leave a legacy of wealth and training and coaching that helps not only my four nephews and my two nieces but other people as well. I prefer to empower other people to have the skills and confidence to create what they want in their lives. I love helping people. And It is very important to me to make a difference by helping offer education so others can make wiser decisions. At my funeral, I will be looking down listening to people say, "Wow, she really helped a lot of people because of her big heart!"

Landon Stokoe

Landon Stokoe is a force to be reckoned with in real estate investing. Landon successfully ran his own contracting business for 25 years. When he learned how to invest in real estate instead of just fixing up houses, there was no holding him back. Within a short period of time, he's made real estate investing his full time career.

Between the fix and flips he's completed, or the buy and hold strategies he's added to his portfolio, he's completed over 20+ real estate deals. At any given time, Landon and his team work on between five to ten properties.

Life wasn't always easy for Landon, but after some trials in his personal life and finding the right career path for long-term success, Landon now enjoys his time finding the next great real estate deal and traveling with his family. Landon is married with two beautiful children, and he now gets to spend much more quality time with them.

Landon finds great satisfaction in sharing his knowledge and expertise with others who share the same passion. He loves showing others how he found the way to financial freedom and helping others get started on that same path.

Shannon:
What inspired you to get into real estate?

Landon:
That's a great question. It started when I lost my hero & the man I looked up to and respected with all of my being. My step dad, Jesus H Valdez, passed away when I was 14. This one event rocked my soul as a kid and forever changed the way I looked at the world. I remember asking my mom, "what do we do now?" Dad was gone, he was the bread winner and main provider for our family. I realized that when he was gone we didn't have much to show for. We had a car that was worth a few thousand dollars and the furniture in our house could have been sold at a yard sale for $1000. I said to my mom, "I don't get it, Dad's been working his entire life, and we don>t have any money in the bank?" Nothing to show for it! And, she's like, "No." So at a young age, I realized that my dad had worked his entire life so we could survive, and from that point forward it kind of scared me in a good way. Reality was in full effect.

Shannon:
Right.

Landon:
I realized, Everyone I knew was doing this same plan. The majority of people are working to get a pay check and trading their time for money and not focusing on building their net-worth and generating monthly cash flow—they're just surviving day to day. If they had a couple bad months, a layoff, less hours per week at work, medical issues, car troubles, or a family death like I had in my life, most people would start to struggle in their personal finances. A house that they had been making payments on for many many years could go into foreclosure for lack of a few payments even if they paid the previous 10 years without missing one payment. Something was just wrong with that equation. I realized the wealthy families held their wealth in real estate and played by a different set of rules. The poor folk mentality is they are playing life on a checkers board moving one

space at time; the wealthy folks are playing on the same board, but they are playing chess. Moving across the board in many different directions and playing by a different set of rules—which gives them the upper hand on accelerating their financial position.

Shannon:
Right.

Landon:
At the age of 14 I did not understand all the concepts of real estate or investing, but I knew that's where I needed to play! Trying to figure out the right path has been a journey.

Shannon:
Okay. So, you were 14 when your step dad passed away.

Landon:
Yeah,14, I always get a little blurry about the small details of my childhood.

Shannon:
Isn't it funny how that happens?

Landon:
Yeah, I was kind of a lost back then, you know. It was like, "Hey, what just happened, my whole world just got spun upside down."

Shannon:
Right. So, if you think back to that self, before he passed away, what did you want to be, what did you want to do?

Landon:
I wanted to be a professional boxer. My dad trained me since I was a young boy. We would have family BBQs all the time, and my family and friends would box each other just for fun. Later in my life I was fortunate enough to be trained by Gene, Jay, and Don Fullmer.

Gene Fullmer was the 1957 middleweight champion of the world. Jay Fullmer was a professional fighter with 125 fights in his career, and Don fought nine world championships & won an American middleweight championship in 1965. Being coached & trained from these boxing legends, along with Nick Butterfield, I won the Utah Golden Gloves championship. Which was a great accomplishment for me. I have awesome memories of those day. My dad was also a drummer in a band. So being around the vibes of a rock band was very fun and high energy. Because of this I also wanted to be in the music and entertainment business. I started a hip hop group called 2 Hype Productions. A couple of friends and I recorded some tracks & started preforming concerts for many major artist & groups of that period of time.

Shannon:
Okay. So, you said that you lost your way, and eventually you got into real estate, what did you do in between?

Landon:
When I was 14 I got a job working for a painting contractor. I worked in that profession for the next 4 years, and at the age of 18 I took the test to become the youngest licensed contractor at that time in the state of Utah. So as soon as I turned 18 I went into business and started my own painting company.

I had to grow up quick and learn fast. I started to ask a lot of questions to other professionals and business owners and learn from their successes and failures.

Shannon:
Right.

Landon:
I opened my first construction company at the age of 18, and I started going down that path because I knew that I wanted to own a business. I wanted to try to at least design a system or be part of a system that could generate cash flow. I did that for about 20 years, plus.

Shannon:

So, do you think that has helped you with your real estate investing? Having that knowledge?

Landon:

Yes. Because being in business, you start learning that there's a lot of different things you can take advantage of as a business owner. Taxes for instance; there are certain things you can do, owning a business and controlling a business versus being a W-2 employee having a job and being controlled There's just different tax benefits you get as a business owner, different opportunities open up for you.

Running my business I met some pretty amazing people along my path. So it expanded my network, it got me used to talking to people and learning how to negotiate. The more you expand your network the greater the possibilities to expand your net-worth become. I feel like I've been conditioning myself for real estate my entire life.

Shannon:

Right.

Landon:

It's definitely helped me out.

Shannon:

When you began your real estate investing career, how important was it to you to either establish your team to help you be successful or that you already had a team established?

Landon:

This is something I talk about frequently. Real estate is not a single person business. It's a team sport. If I went into business and tried doing this by myself, it would have been very tough. So, I realized that the foundation of my business was a key factor in building stability and future momentum. Having the right team members plays a major part of this equation. The foundation of any business is truly important; establish those relationships with people you know so you can call on them when you need them.

At the same time, putting them all together where we can work together and create a synergy. There's something to be said about that. You get a bunch of people chasing down one path or going toward one goal, you seem to get there faster.

Shannon:

In your real estate business, how do you help other people learn more about real estate?

Landon:

You know, first part is that I'm able to tell my story and the paths I've been down already. I messed up a lot, right? I think that was a huge part. When I'm talking with other people and I'm trying to explain to them the concept of real estate, the business of real estate, I'm letting them know, "Look, not everything is going to be perfectly planned in any business. You're going to have hurdles, you're going to have things that just happen that side track you. But you need to make up your mind to weather the storm, all the way through it." When challenges happen, just say, "Hey, you know what, that's part of the game. This is part of the business." And understand that's just of the process and keep pushing forward.

When I'm talking to people about real estate, I would say, just do it right! Do it clean! And have fun along the way! The people that you're building relationships with are going to be part of your story and journey. They will keep coming back to your business. People do business with individuals they like and trust, over, and over, and over. It's not like a one-trick pony where you do one deal with them and they're gone. Take care of your relationships. Take care of your people that you're working with. They might bring you 1 house, 1 deal that could turn into 30 or 40 or 100 deals. You never know. While you're building a business just treat people right and push forward.

Shannon:

That's great advice. In fact, it leads into the next section: if someone was going to get started in real estate investing, and they came to you for advice, what would you recommend that they do first?

Landon:

I would tell them to get educated and get around somebody that's doing that business. Be around somebody that's already involved or someone that can connect them with other professionals. You don't want to remake mistakes that people have already made. Go learn from somebody who's already been in the business a little bit. Go learn from somebody who has already had some failures and many successes.

Ask tons of question, right? Spend time with the people that are doing this kind of a business—go to dinner with them, go spend time with them. Hang out. Pick their brains. Start seeing the culture that they're involved in. Once you spend some time around them, it's the craziest thing, you start becoming that person. You start replicating their style and the things they do! you pick and choose what you want from each person, but all of a sudden, you're doing the same things that they're doing. I say, be influenced by the right people!

I have a saying about being influenced by a certain groups of people: The people that you hang around with most, eventually your Attitude, Thinking, Habits, and Income start replicating those individuals' profiles. So, surround yourself around people that you want to be like. Surround yourself around people that are where you want to be, and run with them!

Shannon:
You are who you hang out with.

Landon:
Yes.

Shannon:
We've all heard that saying or birds of a feather flock together.

Landon:
Yes. Or if you want to run with the big dogs you're going to have to get off the porch. Lol

Shannon:

Let's say you're at dinner with someone and they're picking your brain, because you're the expert. What advice would you give to someone who is allowing fear to hold them back from starting in their real estate investing?

Landon:

Fear is going to always hold people back. I would let them know I was scared when I first started. I think the unknown is always scary. I would talk about the benefits of being a real estate investor and owning rental real estate and doing fix & flips. How to generate massive & passive income. Massive income from doing fix & flips and passive income from collecting rents from properties. which is a faster way to retirement verses traditional methods. And how to do all of this with none of their own money or credit. I would ask them about the current strategy they are using for building wealth and retirement. Then I would talk about what I am doing and encourage them to investigate further. But it comes down to their WHY! If their WHY is great enough it doesn't matter the obstacles or challenges that are in front of them. Once they understand real estate can benefit them and their family for generations, I let them make their own decision if this is right for them.

Understanding the concepts and strategies of real estate investing and what it can do is a key to retiring early. That fear is going to hold you back. Real estate is such a powerful tool. If they're not involved in real estate and they're not pursuing down this path, usually, the outcome of their lives, wherever they're heading in their career, will be working until they're 60 or 65, 70. Their fear is going to push them into that. There are people around me that are free from their jobs, people that live a different life style, because they went and conquered their fears.

It's such a game changer, to know that you can enjoy every single day.

You still do the work and it's still business and you work hard, but it's a different world. So, by conquering my fears I'm able to spend time with my kids. I pick my kids up from school. I'm always going on trips now, I'm not inside of the office anymore. I'm just kind of free and floating around and meeting people. I think about if I never conquered my fears or I never ran down this path, I would be stuck and my fear would have held me back and not let me truly experience my life the way I'm doing it now. Which to me would be a shame.

Shannon:

That's really refreshing to hear. Let's say somebody came to you, and you're at your dinner, and they look at you and they said, "Well, you know, I'm watching the news and we have a new president, and I don't want to get started yet because who knows what the economy is going to do." Do you feel like real estate investing success is dependent on a strong economy?

Landon:

It's always nice if the economy's moving forward and it is strong, but the cool thing is, if you have the right knowledge, the right expertise, and the right mindset of real estate, you can make money in a up or down economy. In every angle of the economy. It doesn't matter what the economy's doing. You know when it goes down more millionaires are made, when the economy drops. Think about '08 and '09, a lot of people talked about everybody losing money, their homes, many people went into foreclosure, they lost their life savings. A lot of people lost money, but that money didn't evaporate into thin air. Someone or some entity made a lot of money.

You start learning these concepts. Being a real estate investor, you start realizing you can help people. There's a lot of people out there struggling, going through real estate challenges. When the economy drops, you're there to help them. You can show them different ways and different angles to save their house or put them in a different situation or help them recapture some of the equity before losing it to the bank.

Shannon:

Elaborate on that for me. What are some of the strategies that you can use to help someone who is potentially going to lose their house to the bank?

Landon:

If somebody's facing foreclosure and an auction date is set, what's their alternative? Some people don't have the financial wherewithal to even fix the situation or the knowledge. Let's just say they had $100,000 in equity. Instead of losing $100,0000 in equity to the bank at auction and destroying the rest of their credit, somebody with the right knowledge of real estate and the right financial wellbeing can step in and say, "Hey, look. Instead of losing your house to foreclosure, I can help! I could actually help you out with the mortgage payments. You can deed me your house, I can give you a certain amount of money depending how much equity the property has."

You make it a win/win for these people, right? Instead of losing everything, they can recapture some of their equity, you can pay the mortgage payment, which I do quite often. Now you're making the payment on their home. The mortgage stays in place and you pick up some equity from the house, which is a deal for you, and it's good business. The home owners' credit is already damaged because they missed payments, but you stop them from going into foreclosure which damages their credit even more. You do damage control for these people.

This is just one strategy. There is a bunch of different strategies you can use, but being able to solve their problems, being able to alleviate their stress, is an excellent way to help the real estate deal move forward. Instead of losing the house to the bank, we'll come in and just pay the house off and still give them some extra money if there is enough equity in the house. The cool thing about doing what we do is we can close on a house fast. We don't have to qualify through a bank and wait two or three months. As an investor, we can buy the house in a few days and stop the foreclosure process.

Shannon:

Would there ever be a time when it is better for you for that house to go to auction, as an investor? Do you pick up homes at auction ever?

Landon:

Auction is not my forte. I pick them up before the auction. There's different strategies, and that's the cool thing about real estate. When

I first started real estate, I used to think, "Oh, you buy a house, or sell a house." What more to it is there? Then you realize when you get inside the real estate world that there are a bunch of different strategies that you can use: 'subject to," short sales, lease options, buy & holds, fix & flips etc.

Shannon:

Go back to when you said that you can have a home owner deed you their home and then you step into their mortgage. What is that called? What strategy is that?

Landon:

That is a subject to strategy or seller financing. I love that strategy. It's one of my favorites actually.

Shannon:

That's why I asked. That sounds like it's one of your favorites because you said you do that quite often. And after you started talking about short sells. Explain to me what a short sale is and why you would use that strategy versus and 'subject to.'

Landon:

A short sale is when a bank will take less then owed for a property. When I was contractor, I took a stated loan on my house. What happened in this process, I lost my house to foreclosure in the bubble when it crashed. I bought a house that, when the market was going up, it was good. When the market went down, my property value dropped dramatically. Now I was under water in this house. My mortgage payment accelerated higher by the way the bank structured me in this ARM loan. When the value of my house went down, I owed more than the house was worth and was behind on payments.

When somebody's in that situation, where there's no equity left in the house, they will do a strategy called a short sale. They have no other option. Nobody's is going to buy a house that's under water or upside down unless they are emotionally involved

We would talk to the bank on behalf of the owner and we will negotiate a short sale on their behalf. Sometimes you can work amazing deals with the bank. I'll tell you what one of my investor friends was able to do. They found a person that was months behind on their house payment. They owed about $197,000 and the house value was only 203K A realtor friend said, "Hey, I have done short sales for fifteen years; let me do the short sell process." My investor friend said thanks for the offer, but they are working with this other guy who's very knowledgeable on short sells as well. He goes, "I'll tell you exactly what is going to happen. The bank has a threshold, they have their limit. They might negotiate the house down to $170,000, $175,000, and that's it, they're not going to go any lower. My friend told the realtor that the investor friend was still going do it. The investor ended up negotiating the deal around 127k.

Shannon:

Wow!

Landon:

My friends let the realtor know, "Hey! It took a littlelonger, we're into it like eight or nine months, but he negotiated it for around $127,000!" He says, "No way. That has to be a fluke. They don't do that. How' did he do it? How did he get the price so low?" The investor said, "Specialized knowledge."

Shannon:

Right.

Landon:

There are lot of people doing short sales, they've been doing them forever, but there are other strategies that you can apply to the short sells and actually help make your own equity position. I've watched it done, I've been apart of these deals, and all of a sudden you can take a deal that's under water, that has no equity and make a good return on it. Opportunities are not always found. Sometimes they're created.

Shannon:

That's awesome. You said that it took a little bit longer to get it to that low price?

Landon:

Yes.

Shannon:

How long does a short sell usually take from beginning to end? Because by the sound of it, it sounds like you need to get out of it quickly, so do the short sales, and get out quickly.

Landon:

It's so funny, they call it short sales but they should be called extra-long sale. Short sells often take a while.

Shannon:

In the meantime, if you have short sells on your desk, would you start looking for fix and flips?

Landon:

Yes! Exactly that. I always say this, have the right knowledge and the right strategies. Deals are not always found, sometimes the deal is created or structured.

Shannon:

Expand on that. How do you create a deal?

Landon:

When I'm talking with a homeowner and they're going to lose a house, normally they're just going to lose the house. But we get to go in and negotiate, "Hey here's an option you could do," we're negotiating the deal to what we want it to be and coming to terms with those people. On a short sell, there's some tactics that you can do to create the deal.

I was telling you about my friend, who said he's been doing it for 15 years and said there was no way to bring it down. But there's a way of negotiating, there's a way of processing paperwork that helps you increase your chances of getting more equity in a deal. It's all strategies, right? Everything's a strategy in real estate.

Shannon:

Expand on one of those strategies—what are a couple of the strategies you're going to lay out for me?

Landon:

I'll explain a house that I've actually done.

Shannon:

Perfect.

Landon:

A homeowner was going to go into foreclosure, and I ended up spending around $9000 on this deal. That was just to catch their mortgage current. What I did for them, I said, "Look, let's keep your existing mortgage in place. And I will make the payments for now on." The cool thing is, the mortgage payment was around the $950 a month. Now, I could have bought this house and just flipped it and made some money and been done, but I want passive income though rental real estate, which I love. I ended up buying this house, I spent $9,000 to bring the existing mortgage payments current, with around $120,000 still being owed on the property. The cool thing is, the house value in about $210,000. This means I stepped into a large amount of equity.

Shannon:

Perfect.

Landon:

A property management company rents this house out for $1,700 a month. This property produces positive cash flow every month.

Shannon:

Wow!

Landon:

After you pay a management fee, your taxes and everything else, you're in a cash flow position around $600 per month. Now, every month, I have steady money coming in. Once I did that, I realized I could go structure more deals like this one. Imagine doing 10 to 20 houses with that strategy using none of your own money or credit? This is why rental real estate is an awesome way to get out of the rat race. A lot of people go and work their 40-40-40 plan, they work 40 hours a week, for 40 years to retire, off of 40 percent of what they can't even survive off of already.

Shannon:
Right.

Landon:
I want to enjoy my life while I'm still young enough and while I can still enjoy hiking and spending time with my family and my kids. I realized, if I do enough of these houses, I could have cash flow coming in every month. Maybe it's $5,000 a month, maybe it's $12,000 a month, but that's retirement to me. Controlling money instead of money controlling me. At the end of the month instead of waiting, thinking "Oh, I've need to make money now. I got to pay my bills at the end of the month," when the end of the month comes you're getting richer as you're getting older. You look forward to the end of the month. It's a different strategy and a different mindset from what I was brought up with. Once you're in that position, clarity happens. You can start helping other people achieve results and this is why I love real estate. It's a people business. And you get to help others.

Shannon:
Are you looking into moving into multi-family?

Landon:
When you're doing single family, it's one deal and you can make a good equity position or good cash flow position off that one house. But realize when you're buying an apartment complex, it's still one purchase, it's still one deal. So, instead of buying the house, we can buy the apartment complex and now we have multiple people paying rents. Let's just say for instance we have a 16-plex; if 2 people can't

pay rent, you still have 14 other people paying every month. The cash flow is greater. The security is greater because of all the money coming in. When you understand money and the way that money works, you can start using that cash flow and that extra money as velocity. Which is another topic.

Shannon:

Well, go into it. You can start using that cash flow from multi-family dwellings cause it's a positive cash flow. So now that's your velocity for other deals. What is the risk in that?

Landon:

There's always a risk. But the more you know about a particular subject you can minimize your risk.

Shannon:

So, you got positive cash flow but just enough. So, that might not be worth the risk to use that positive cash flow towards another investment, but it may be worth it to use it to keep a couple of units empty and refurbish them. How could you use that money in both high risk and low risk and why would you do it that way?

Landon:

Here's the other thing, I guess I should say this, as an investor, before I step into a property or an apartment complex or anything, I usually picking my property up with equity existing in them. I don't buy on the retail market. I'm usually negotiating that down or I'm not buying it. I go after houses & buildings that have equity potential.

For instance, I had a deal on the table for $1.1 million and I just had to buy the deal, but the terms of the deal didn't work out for me. So, I actually walked away from that because there wasn't enough equity and the risk of cash flow coming in was not there. It was too minuscule for the deal. So I have thresholds that I set in place and where I got to have a certain amount of money coming in. If all these numbers don't fit my box, I don't do the deal.

Shannon:

Okay.

Landon:

I learned this concept in real estate investing "to fall in love with the numbers not the deal."

Shannon:

Is that number always the same for you?

Landon:

Yeah. Most of the time, but it depends if there is equity; maybe you're in the equity deal and you›re looking at flipping an apartment complex. I would move on it for that manner. Maybe there's not a lot of equity, but it is a lot of cash flow. It still makes it a deal. Cash flow is key in the business.

Shannon:

Why?

Landon:

When money is constantly coming in, you can keep things moving. Especially if it's real cash flow, not just extra money to pay a bill, it's not making $5000 and spending $5000. It's making $5000 and spending only $2,500. The remaining is extra cash flow. Without it, your business is dead. It dries up. You need to have cash flow coming in. That's what keep the business alive.

Shannon:

Is cash flow important in all businesses or just real estate?

Landon:

All businesses need cash flow to survive. If you don't have it, your business is over with. Most businesses can only sustain a certain amount of time, usually three to six months. Especially a lot of new businesses. I think that's why a lot of new businesses fail. They're still learning the ropes and learning strategies, and they go into business and they don't have enough cash flow coming in and they don't have enough money or credit to survive the business through the beginning stages. Which is always the toughest time because you need to get your name out there.

Shannon:

You started in single family, now you're looking into multi-family. Most millionaires and billionaires have investments in commercial real estate. Do you think that you will move into commercial real estate? If yes, why? And if no, why?

Landon:

Real estate is real estate, right? If the right opportunity presents itself and the numbers make sense, I'll do the deal. I want to get familiar and get marinated with each strategy. I want to become an expert in houses. Then become the expert in apartments. I believe that doing commercial real estate is just the next chapter. You start playing with different amounts of money as different risk tolerances. Houses are usually a smaller number compared to apartments and commercial buildings, I would say get involved, get moving forward, but my mindset is I crawl before I walk. If I made a mistake on a house in the beginning, I could recoup after that. Just making small moves and making strategies. As I go forward, I let my knowledge build up and acclimate to that business. Commercial is definitely on my to-do list.

Shannon:

Last question, and we touched on it a little bit at the beginning where you talked about your step dad working hard and then having to grow up and you having to pay bills and help with your mom. What type of legacy do you want to leave? So you built this successful contracting business, worked your rear off for years for that, and now you are transitioning into real estate. Why? What is the legacy that you want to leave behind?

Landon:

Once again, it goes back to doing what we did as kids, right? I really believe that children learn what they live. When I was kid, most of my family just did what grandma and grandpa did. They passed what they knew down and did the best they could. The knowledge that was given to me was go to school, get education to get a job, to become an employee, or go get a career, but usually it would lead to becoming an employee. The problem with that was, you start off in the worst tax bracket, right off the get go! For my kids, my son Dax and my beautiful daughter Koya, they're still young at this point. My son's ten and my daughter's five. Look, life's not getting any easier if you're just working a job. It's getting tougher and most people can barely make it. I look at my kids and I say, "Hey, I want you to be who you want to be. I want you to be the person that you can excel to be." I still want them to learn the ethics of working hard and being respectful and know what it is to have to survive. The legacy behind what I'm doing, what I'm putting together, is giving them different knowledge. Giving them wealthy knowledge about paying taxes, owning & controlling businesses, owning rental real estate. My son walks my fix and flips with me. He runs the numbers already. He could fill out a financial spread sheet. He gets it! He gets it better than most adults. He's understanding cash flow & leveraging.

The conversations from me being around this environment of entrepreneurs and wealthy mindset individuals is absolutely awesome, it is constantly feeding into their minds. He's understanding business, money, interest. He's understanding how I operate and run a business. The legacy for me is when I die my kids could take over my business or build their own empire from applying these actions and strategies in their lives. From this part forward, they will own houses, they can inherit it down, and I can control this all through my family trust that we set up and allow my kids to live a different life than most people. For me, quality of life is huge. It's one of the biggest things for me. It kills me because a lot of people aren't living up to their true potential quality of life that they should be. They're trapped by a job. They're trapped by just surviving. My kids have this opportunity to propel their lives and then give it to their kid's kids. So the decisions I'm making right now are not just for me, they're for my family for generations. I can change the outcome of the way they live their lives. At the same time, we influence other people and other friends and other people's family to do the same. We create a ripple to change many people's lives. We are giving them knowledge. We're helping them get to that next level; we're helping them understand financial strategies; we're showing them how real estate can get you free! When you learn the right strategy to pick up houses, you start realizing and you're building net worth and wealth.

I worked my life away for 20+ years to survive. What I've been able to do in real estate in the last few years has trumped my entire previous career. Get yourself in a better position so you can help others do the same and make the world a better place for people who would never know your name. Quality of life and FREEDOM is what I'm fighting for.

Pat Walley

Investing in America one Property at a Time

Americas Property Investors

Pat, a Colorado native, is passionate about God, Family, and Real Estate. He joined the US Navy Nuclear Power Program at age 17 and served his country for 9½ years, wrapping up his career as a decorated instructor in the SF Bay area. In 1992, Pat entered corporate America and subsequently received dozens of awards, bonuses, and top honors. He innovated several training programs and excelled in simplifying tough tech-speak and mentoring fellow employees.

Real Estate investing is the vehicle he has chosen to replace the 20+ year IT career. In 2015, he aligned himself with one of the fastest growing companies in the US. His team of investors, his portfolio of assets, and his income continues to grow. He trains and collaborates with other investors around the country. Pat is the current president of his local chapter of Gideons International, member of his Local Chamber of Commerce, and a leader in his church. He married his high school sweetheart and resides in Folsom, CA.

"The idea of becoming financially successful while helping others has always been my dream and Real Estate Investing is making that dream a reality."

Shannon:

What inspired you to get into real estate investing?

Pat:

I have worked in corporate America for several years, and was pretty much at the end of my rope with the whole IT industry phenomenon. I was getting burned out.

Shannon:

Okay. You woke up one morning and said, "Here I am."

Pat:

I've actually been interested in real estate for several years. I just didn't realize there was an opportunity to be an investor. I was looking for the right one. I met somebody, and things went well, and here I am.

Shannon:

Several people say, "I met somebody. I ran into somebody." They make it almost sound like fate. Is that what happened to you? Were you in an elevator and you ran into someone? Were you driving down the street?

Pat:

I don't like using the word "fate." Success is when preparation and hard work intersects with opportunity. I had been preparing for that opportunity, so that when it did arrive, I knew it. That's pretty much what happened. I had been searching for an answer, wanting to be in real estate investing but I didn't know anything about it, and I needed to find someone that did. I met James Leis and his team of investors. I knew right away that I was aligned with the right people.

Shannon:

That's awesome. Tell me the story of where or how you met James.

Pat:

I actually saw a roadside sign that said, "Successful Real estate investor seeking apprentice." That word "apprentice" popped out as that's exactly what I needed—an opportunity to lean the business from an expert. I called my wife right away and told her "I found it!" I was so excited. Funny thing is, the sign was gone the next day, so God put me in the right place at the right time.

Shannon:
Wow.

Pat:
I called the number, answered a few questions, and requested a follow-up call. James called me the next morning and shared his story with me. We both had military background and are both men of faith. We just hit it off immediately and his success was what I had been looking for in my life. I went to his office the next day and he invited me to join his team. I think a critical component in any success whether it's sports, or business, relationships is to be part of a winning team.

Shannon:
Perfect. If someone was going to start in real estate, and came to you for advice, what would you recommend that they do first?

Pat:
That was almost like a segue, wasn't it?

Shannon:
Yes, it was.

Pat:
Honestly, align yourself with a good mentor. I've heard this for years. With anything, find someone that's doing what I want to do, whether it'd be lifestyle, money, where they're living, etc. Then, if they're doing it the way I want to do it, follow their footsteps and copy them. If they're successful the way that I determine success to be, then there's a good chance that I'll become successful too.

Shannon:

Yeah. I love that you preface the word "success." That's actually when I'm interviewing people to hire in my business, one of the interview questions I ask them is, do you consider yourself successful? I have some people that are extremely successful by all worldly standards that will say, "Of course, I do." I also have the 19-year-old kid, that by the definition of the word success, he's sleeping on his friend's coach.

Pat:

Right? Hey, I'm on my own!

Shannon:

That's right. He'll look at me and say, "Yeah, I'm successful. I moved out of my parents' house. I'm taking a class in college. I'm getting a job." I love that you defined success as the way that you see success to be.

Shannon:

Okay. You were talking about this team. You were talking about mentors. You spoke a little bit about James. How has mentors, in your real estate investing, helped you to navigate potential pitfalls?

Pat:

That's a great question. Real estate investing is not for the faint of heart. Let's get that out there right away. It takes courage to be a real estate investor.

Shannon:

Yes, it does.

Pat:

I'm going to revert to the military because I'm a big supporter of military vets. I'm a veteran. I come from a family of veterans. Success comes from many moving parts operating as one. Mentorship is like going through a minefield and having someone with a map leading me through the minefield. If I trust them, and follow their footsteps, there's a good chance I am going to make it out the other side alive. Having that mentorship, and forming the relationship, and being able to see behind the scenes and little nuances, it is all so critical to success in any endeavor. If I want to learn to make more money in real estate, it only makes sense to follow the leadership of someone who is already where I want to be.

Shannon:

Great. Tell me a time about in your... You said you had how many years in corporate America? 20?

Pat:
And then some.

Shannon:

Okay. As you get into real estate investing, tell me a time that a mentor in your corporate career has given you advice that's really helped you or saved you from a pitfall, and possibly lead you in the direction of knowing that you want to be in real estate investing full time?

Pat:

I have had so many amazing mentors in my life. My first exposure to Real Estate Investing was while I was working for a global digital imaging company. I was new in the industry and my supervisor took me under his wing and taught me the ropes. He helped me learn the system and brought me up to speed. He showed me how to work efficiently and saved me from countless hours of 'fixing mistakes'. He was one of the few people I ever met who could outwork me. Greg also had rental properties and had a plan to replace his 18-year career income with the money he was making in real estate. I guess that is when I REALLY caught the bug.

Shannon:

One of the ways that I word it is some people have their forever home. Some people have their forever job. Sometimes, people have a forever lifestyle. You meet other people and they're afraid. They know what they want to be better. What advice would you give someone who is wanting to make changes, but is allowing fear to hold them back in starting their real estate investing?

Pat:

I can only speak to my fear. I reached a point where I realized I had become part of the 40/40/40 plan. I had agreed to work 40 hrs./week (at least) for 40 years to retire on 40% of what I was making. THAT scared me and then it was just a matter of which fear was bigger?

Shannon:

That's okay. What advice would you give if they came to you and said, "My gosh. What should I do?"

Pat:

I would say, do it anyway. Do it afraid.

Shannon:

That's a perfect answer. That's a perfect answer. Then, you would probably say to them, "I'll help you."

Pat:

Sure. How many times have we had a similar situation, we ended up having to go through the situation and look back and say, "That wasn't so bad." I heard something once and have used it often: Fear is something small that casts a big shadow.

Shannon:

I like that. I've never actually heard that one.

Pat:

It's always better on the other side of fear. If God be for me, who can be against me?

Shannon:

Perfect. Let's say they come to you and they say, "I'd really like to get started but here we are at this time of our lives, a new president was just elected. The economy is shaky. I just don't know if this is the right time. Our economy is just not that strong." Do you feel that real estate investing success is dependent on a strong economy?

Pat:

It's not dependent on a strong economy. It works better sometimes. A strong economy is just a perception. Successful real estate investors make money whether the economy is up or down. If it's going up, the prices are going up. I have a house, and it's gaining value as I am rehabbing it. When it's down, there's more discounted properties available. People need a place to live. There's always opportunities for success in real estate.

Shannon:

Perfect. Tell me about a real estate strategy, maybe a home acquisition strategy that you could use and would create the most success in a strong economy.

Pat:

In a strong economy?

Shannon:

Uh-huh (affirmative). A question because you were talking about when you're rehabbing a home, you're gaining value as you're rehabbing.

Pat:

Right. Yeah, on a strong economy or a growing economy, definitely, fix and flip is awesome. A multi-family/apartment building is even better because, then, I'm multiplying my profits with cashflow. Yeah, I would say that—fix and flip. The acquisition strategies vary. The best one is just somebody who wants to get rid of a property, and signs it over to you for a fraction of what it's worth, or better yet, free! That's always the best one. It's cash deal. It's quick.

Shannon:

All right. Elaborate on that for me. You just made it sound like there are people out there who have a home, and they go, "Sure, go ahead and take this off my hands." Does that actually happen?

Pat:

Shannon, the biggest surprise that I had when I started real estate investing is that people don't necessarily need top dollar for their property. I always had the mindset of a real estate agent selling it on the market trying to get the best price. There's so many situations that the solution to the problem is more important than the price. A tired landlord is a great example. They're a real estate investor, multiple properties, and maybe he's just got one that's just a little far out of his comfort zone for traveling or whatever. There's a lot of different reasons. As a good negotiator, I solve their problem and get a cash flowing property at a deep discount. How awesome is that?

Shannon:

You keep talking about cash flow. What is cash flow? Why is it important?

Pat:

Simply put, Cash Flow is proceeds from a performing asset after all expenses and taxes. It's important because this IS the passive income I want. Money coming in regardless of my physical participation. It doesn't matter whether it's a $5 million acquisition or a $50,000 acquisition. It's profits above and beyond the expenses of owning that asset.

Shannon:

Being in California where real estate is some of the most expensive in the nation, you just talked about the $5 million or $50,000, that's true. Cash flow is king. If it's positive, it's positive. Does it scare you at all to start looking, when you're looking at your deals, you're looking at deals that are half a million dollars versus, say, someone in Texas who can buy a house for $50,000. Is that dollar amount being in California intimidating to you?

Pat:

It's not intimidating because, it's really just a numbers game. If the numbers work, then they just work. I am reviewing some properties in the Midwest with $500 a month cashflow. Here, in California, that doesn't even pay for gas money!

Shannon:
That doesn't even cover the HOAs.

Pat: Right. **The formulas are still the same whether they're small or large numbers. Do you have the guts to get behind the wheels of a sports car? You know?**

Shannon:
Yes, I do.

Pat:
That's why it's addicting. It's addicting to get out there in the game. It becomes so fun and exciting. It's adrenalin. There's a lot of work, but it's definitely a lot of fun.

Shannon:
Good. Have you ever considered investing in other areas of the country? If so, what would you need to do that successfully?

Pat:
Absolutely. I am actually in the process of acquiring some property in Oklahoma. I've got family in Oklahoma, so it is a nice tax write off when I visit. It's good to have someone that I trust that knows the market as an investing partner or guide. As part of a nationwide organization, I have the inside scoop, if you will.

Shannon:
Great. Thank you. Let's go back to the economy question. We talked about a strong economy, and we just talked about several things that you can do to invest in a strong economy. Let's say, heaven forbid, 2008 happens again tomorrow, what real estate investing strategy would you use if we were in a weak economy or an economy where the real estate bubble bursts?

Pat:
That would be bad to have 2008 happen again.

Shannon:

Yes. Yes, it would.

Pat:

The subject-to strategy becomes very common. People are losing their homes. I'm able to step in, provide a way to stop the foreclosure, possibly save them from bankruptcy, and regain some dignity and help them get settled into a new residence.

Shannon:

You started to elaborate our subject-to. Elaborate on that for me. To what?

Pat:

Subject to existing financing. The owner deeds the property to me, I take over and make payments to the lending institution. I never assume the loan. No banks, no credit required, fast close, and I control the property and can rent it or do a lease-option.

Shannon:

When you have a subject-to loan, is that also commonly known as a seller finance? Are they the same thing?

Pat:

It's not the same thing. In a seller finance, the seller owns the property outright.

Shannon:

I didn't know that. They're similar, but not-

Pat:

For the subject-to, I'm making the mortgage payments, rather my tenant, but the previous owner keeps the loan. I have helped them avoid foreclosure and am helping them rebuild their credit and someone else is paying my payment and eventually paying off my new house. That is Real Estate Investing at it's best!

Shannon:

Got it.

Pat:

I actually did a seller finance transaction for a personal property.

Shannon:

Really?

Pat:

Yes. The man owned it outright. He agreed to finance our purchase of the property. We made payments to him. I had a good, beautiful house at a pretty reasonable rate. I didn't have to come up with a lot of money down, and I was able to move in quickly. It took less than a month and did not have to use a bank or provide a credit check. Again, very little money, no credit.

Shannon:

That's awesome. Speaking of quickly, what do you know about short sale?

Pat:

I personally know about them. Not enough to talk about them.

Shannon:

That's okay. How about lease options?

Pat:

Lease options, yes.

Shannon:

All right, perfect. As a real estate investor, how can an individual benefit from lease options? Is that something that you can combine with another investment strategy to have two or three strategies in place at the same time?

Pat:

That's the fun part about this is the more that I learn about it, the more that I participate. It's like having a batman tool belt. I reach out, and here's another one. This works. This works. I need the grappling hook and the gun, bam! A lease option is a really great transaction. I always have to make sure that I'm in compliance with the local laws.

Lease option is a great way to help somebody or a family that may be having a difficult time getting financing. It's like having a renter, but they get the pride of ownership because the whole principle behind lease option is that they're leasing the property with the option to buy. They are not just a tenant then. It gives a lot of flexibility depending on how I acquired the property. I purchase a property with subject-to and then lease-option it back to someone. Nice and easy.

Shannon:

Right. You talked about the laws and how different states and different areas have laws on lease options. How can you find that out to make sure you're protected? Do you just go down to the library and research the laws?

Pat:

Google it. No, I'm just kidding. It's imperative, and this is what I have learned through education, is that it's imperative to make sure that I've got an attorney. Let the professionals handle it.

Shannon:

Perfect. As we're talking about professionals and you're talking about building your team and having an attorney, as you continue in your real estate investing career, you have more homes that you're purchasing for buy and hold. You touched a little bit on the price of family dwelling. How does real estate allow you to earn massive income and passive income? Which one is your goal or is the goal both?

Pat:

It's both. Because I'm primarily talking to people in my daily walk that aren't savvy necessarily to real estate investment, but they may be interested in the idea of passive income—what we think of as retirement. From the corporate world, from an employee's standpoint, it's, "If I work enough years, I can put money in my company 401K and maybe buy some stock. When I invest properly, then I can retire and I get a steady check off of whatever interest or however my assets are performing." Of course, what happens if the stock drops or the market turns? I watched close friends lose enough stock and 401K value that they had to keep working after they had what they thought was enough to retire with.

As an investor, a passive income is a great goal for exactly that. My goal is: 10 homes owned free and clear cash flowing $1,000/mo. providing $10,000/mo. cash flow! That's a nice day. Passive income is definitely my goal because I don't want to be working till I am too old to do anything. I want to have that retirement lifestyle. The massive income is making a lot of money on a single transaction sometimes in a very short period of time. Real estate is the only place I know of that the average person can do that.

Shannon:

Awesome. If somebody is starting with little money or poor credit, there's an old saying in corporate America, we keep going back to that because that's my background and yours, people work, and work, and work; yet, they have nothing to show for it. They still have living paycheck to paycheck. If somebody wants to get started in real estate investing, doesn't it take money to make money? If you have very little money or poor credit, how are you supposed to get started.? How are you supposed to make money if you don't have it?

Pat:

That's a great question, Shannon. I think that is probably the one fear that hold most people back. People have told me "I would, but I don't have any money," or "I would, but my credit is bad. I don't qualify to be able to participate in that." I think that's probably the biggest misconception I had as well. I would say that it does take money to make money, however, that money doesn't have to be mine. People borrow money to start businesses every day. We all come to the table with different currencies, but the one currency I have found is paramount is integrity. If you come to the table and you don't have integrity as a currency, then you're probably not going to make it as an investor, or as an employee, or as a father or mother. If you don't have integrity, then the whole game is off. There's so many resources that I didn't know even existed and I learned that I could participate in a real estate transaction using other peoples' resources.

Shannon:

You touched on the integrity piece, which you're right, it's huge, and the relationship piece is huge. I'd like you to elaborate on exactly how. Meaning, you can go to the bank and say, "Look, I have integrity. I want this house. I have no money, but here's a handshake. I promise you, I'll get you your money in six months." The bank is not going to do that for you. Where can you use the integrity currency in order to help you buy a home?

Pat:

Great question. As an investor, my word is my bond. Private lending depends on good numbers and trust. I have access to a lot of money now because I have built a good reputation of doing good business. With the banks, it's the system that was created for the W-2 employee to borrow money. Its based on time on job, credit history and score, taxable income, etc. Here is a great story: I was working with an investor in the SF Bay area who had three properties with a total of $1.5 Million in equity and he couldn't get a loan from the bank to do some acquisition strategies because his books were done right. As a contractor, he didn't show a lot of income because he had a lot of tax deductions. Any business owner understands this. Here's a guy with over $3 million in assets for collateral who couldn't get a loan. I always thought that was really just mind blowing.

The real estate investing system is based on people that have resources and want to invest them to get the best returns possible. Real estate can pretty consistently generate double digit returns. Who wouldn't want that? There's a lot of cash out there.

Shannon:

I would.

Pat:

It's just a matter of knowing how to find it. Imagine borrowing from someone's retirement account to invest in real estate and they make double digit returns. My private lenders are very happy with their returns. The huge untapped resource are IRAs. There's a lot of money in IRAs. People are earning 3%, 4%, 8%, and I'd can help them to be earning 12%, 15%, 18% in some cases.

Shannon:

When you're using people's IRAs, do you have to sign people who are over 62, 64, 66, so that they can actually access that IRA?

Pat:

That would be limiting, wouldn't it?

Shannon:

I see.

Pat:

No, there's a lot different strategies. That's where the education component comes in. This isn't something you just go up, "Let me borrow some money out of the IRA." There's legalities, and definitely being educated, and, again, having a professional to be able to pick up the phone and say, "This is what I'd like to do. This is how I'd like to do it. What's the best way to manage that?" The legal professionals are the first always. Always have a good tax person.

Shannon:

Perfect.

Pat:

I don't have to worry about that because I let them worry about that.

Shannon:

Exactly. Did you read the article that Woody sent to you, the Forbes Magazine article?

Pat:

I did.

Shannon:

All right. According to that article, real estate is one of the top three ways that people become wealthy. As a real estate expert, why do you feel this is the case?

Pat:

People need a place to live. That's a simple fact. Find that need, and fill it, and you'll become wealthy. There's no more land being made. I think that's something that Warren Buffett knew. Now, you see, his real estate company signs everywhere. Follow the leader, right?

Shannon:

Who doesn't want to follow Warren Buffett?

Pat:

Right.

Shannon:

Most millionaires and billionaires do have investments in real estate, but more importantly they have invested in commercial real estate. Why do you think that's important?

Pat:

I used to think commercial real estate was like skyscrapers and strip malls, and it's not just that. There are office parks. They can be multi-family units. There's a lot of different varieties of what we would fall under what we would consider commercial. The simple fact is you get multiple streams of income from the same property.

Shannon:

Which creates positive cash flows. That helps...

Pat:

Shannon, for one house, I get that rent from one tenant. If that tenant moves out and my property is vacant, I've lost 100% of my cash flow. If I have a 50-unit business building or a 50-unit complex, and I lose one tenant, I only lose one-fiftieth maybe of the cash flow.

Shannon:

What legacy do you want to leave?

Pat:

Shannon, of course, living a multigenerational resource for my family. I do want them to have a nice lifestyle and have financial options.

I'm a man of faith. Really, we don't take those things with us. They rust and they fade away. I think if I can leave a legacy of anything, Shannon, it would be sharing hope. I share that with everybody that I come in contact with There's a lot of situations that people think are hopeless—but there is always hope. It's the changed lives that I help leave behind that's a better legacy than any dollar amount I can ever put on a piece of paper. With God, all things are possible.

Charlyne White

Charlyne White is a dedicated, bright and caring woman whose journey is one of inspiration for many young women who dare to chase their dreams. She is from a long family line of entrepreneur women; (her grandmother was cousin to Gladys who owned "Gladys's Luncheonette", a well know soul food restaurant established on Chicago's south side in the mid 1940's). The pioneers before her and the legacies they left behind has become part of the motivating force attributing to her success.

Charlyne White is President at Sip and See, LLC, a company that distributes nutritious beverages nationwide. She leads a group of 156 Women Business Owners in the Northwest Suburbs of Chicago, Illinois, and is a Certified Protocol Officer with The Protocol School of Washington. Her businesses include Heavenly Jet Air Services, a private charter services for an elite clientele and CRW Consulting Firm established to help launch small businesses. Her newest business venture is CRW Business Development Group, focusing on personal development combined with real estate investing.

As her journey continued, she became a financial analyst (contractor) for the Unites States Air Force and broke the barriers as she launched a career in aviation by obtaining her private pilot's license at Comair Aviation Academy and her commercial pilot's license at Avion Air Aviation, both at Orlando-Sanford International Airport, Florida and a career span of 18 years with Delta Airlines.

Charlyne has successfully balanced her personal life and business world with passion and commitment all while continuing training herself toward greater entrepreneur accomplishments.

Shannon:

According to Forbes magazine, real estate is one of the top three ways people become wealthy. As a real estate expert, why do you feel that this is the case?

Charlyne:

Because real estate is one of the basic necessities in life. Unless you are homeless, most people own their home or lease the property. So, real estate provides one of the basic necessities in life. We all need food, water and shelter. Real estate covers one of those.

Shannon:

What inspired you to get into real estate?

Charlyne:

Well, I never really thought I wanted to get into real estate, but I met a woman on an airplane and she was so excited about this real estate investment community that she was involved in, and she asked me three questions that I had never thought about. That intrigued me and I wanted to learn more. I actually thought she was the female Donald Trump or a real estate mogul. She was excited and she was so passionate about what she was doing. And that inspired me to want to learn more.

Shannon:

How does passion help you be a better real estate investor?

Charlyne:

Passion? Well, with anything we do in life, when you're passionate about what you do, you're excited about it, you're comfortable talking to other people about what you do, and you want to share it with the world. So, my passion for real estate investing inspired me to want learn everything I can about real estate investing, which gives me the confidence to share my knowledge with others and add value to as many people as I can.

Shannon:

What is one of the top real estate strategies that you've learned or that you like to use?

Charlyne:

Well, there's so many strategies that I've learned that I haven't actually used yet. But one of them is velocity banking. I love that strategy. I also like the strategy of raising private capital or using other people's money to invest.

Shannon:

How does using other people's money help you become a better investor?

Charlyne:

Well, if I am going to ask someone for money, then I need to show them a plan. That opens up a whole set of other opportunities. I wish someone had asked me that question before my first real estate purchase because I did not know what I did not know, and I lost a lot of money because of that.

Shannon:

How has education helped you in your real estate investing?

Charlyne:

Oh my goodness. Again, I did not know what I didn't know. The strategies that I've learned in this online real estate investment education is second to none. First you start with your investor ID so you learn what kind of person you are, what you're passionate about and then what will motivate you, what strategies you would use. And then when you're talking to people you can speak from authority or from experience because you've learned from the best real estate investment education company.

Shannon:

If someone was going to start in real estate, what would you recommend they do first?

Charlyne:

I would say first start with education. You have to educate yourself. In our online education you would start with learning your investor ID and then you learn different strategies. You build a team and then you network with this investor community that is just awesome and incredible. It has to first start with education.

Shannon:

In your business how do you help other people learn more about real estate?

Charlyne:

When I first approach a person, I simply have a conversation about real estate investing. I ask questions to learn what they are doing. I share some of the strategies that I have learned. I talk about how investing could benefit them or enhance their lives. Then I invite them down to meet this group of people who showed me how to do the same thing.

Shannon:

How has real estate changed your life?

Charlyne:

Well, personally I still live in the same five-bedroom home that I lived in before I was introduced to real estate investing. But with the strategies that are in place, there is no reason that I cannot advance even further than where I am. The real estate investing education gave to the knowledge and confidence I needed to be successful. I talk to more people now and share some of the strategies I have learned. Now that I am a part of this investing community, I can introduce other people to this group of real estate investors. That's what I should be doing.

Shannon:

What are some of the creative ways to acquire property?

Charlyne:

Lease options, seek private lenders, and also seller financing.

Shannon:

If you are starting with little money or poor credit, what are some strategies to get into real estate?

Charlyne:

I would start by raising private capital. Using other people's retirement accounts is a good way to get into real estate with little money or poor credit. Seller financing and lease options are creative ways to acquire properties without using a bank.

Shannon:

Will you explain how that works?

Charlyne:

Sure. Lease options allow a buyer to lease a property for a set period of time with the option to buy the property at the end of a specified period of time. It is like living with someone before marriage or test driving the property if you will while you are looking a creative way to finance it.

Shannon:

What is the number one mistake an individual makes when buying their first real estate investment?

Charlyne:

I would have to say making emotional purchases, not being educated, not going through the numbers to find out if this is a good deal or not. That is what I did.

Shannon:

When you began your real estate investing career, how important was it to establish a team of people to be successful?

Charlyne:

Oh my goodness, I cannot even imagine doing real estate or any type of investing without a team, and that includes coaches and mentors, real estate agents or brokers, and a title company just to name a few. You also need boots on the ground and people that are out looking for properties for you. And your network of real estate investors who understand what it is you do and can add value to your team.

Shannon:

You mentioned coaches and mentors. How have mentors in real estate investing helped you navigate potential pitfalls?

Charlyne:

Wow. Well, because, again, when I purchased my first property I didn't know what I didn't know, and I made a lot of bad decisions. So, starting in real estate, or any venture, coaches and mentors are crucial to my success. These are successful people who have gone before me and have done what I am are trying to do. Having a coach and a mentor allows you to learn from their successes and failures. And then if you're coachable, that is a win-win. You do not have to re-invent the wheel. You just have to be coachable and follow their system.

Shannon:

What advice would you give to someone who is allowing fear to hold them back from starting to invest in real estate?

Charlyne:

Fear? I would say, first of all, face your fears and do it anyway. I have a mentor that said "dragons are real, but they are imaginary. There are bad thoughts in your mind that never come true because they are not true." (Hugh Zaretsky) And then I've even learned a hack from Woody about just focusing because it's not real, it's just all in your head. I had to get rid of negative thinking or what Joyce Meyers calls "that stinking thinking" and just go for it. Educate yourself, have the right group of people around you, build the right team and you'll be fine.

Shannon:

I agree. There's a lot of fear when people think about the economy always going up and down. Does a fluctuating economy really effect real estate?

Charlyne:

Not necessarily. I mean you can succeed in real estate whether the economy is up or down. If you are educated, you know how run the numbers, have several strategies to use, and you know the pitfalls to look for. Yes, you can be successful in a fluctuating economy.

Shannon:

How does real estate allow you to earn massive and passive income?

Charlyne:

Massive and passive income? You can earn massive income or quick money by fixing and flipping properties and build passive income by getting into rentals and developing a portfolio and strategies to do that.

Shannon:

You mentioned passive income. That's the type of cashflow that you get every day from rental properties. Why is that such an important part to real estate investing?

Charlyne:

I've learned through the real estate investing education that buying one rental property a year could generate passive income or generate wealth. If you have a fourplex, one of the units could pay for the mortgage, you could live in one of the units, and the other two units could generate cash flow or passive income. That's a great way to generate wealth.

Shannon:
How do you minimize the risk of investing so that you can maximize your potential success?

Charlyne:
Minimize the risk? I would say education, going through the numbers, learning the pitfalls, learning your investor ID.

Shannon:
What type of legacy do you want to leave?

Charlyne:
I just want people to know how much I really care because at the end of the day, I don't think people really care about who you know or what you know. People really just want to feel like you care. I wish money was more important to me but it isn't. So, at the end of the day I just want people to feel like I really cared, and I hope that I have helped someone just by investing in this real estate investing education myself and sharing my knowledge with others. I hope that I could help a massive amount of people because there are a large number of people who do not know how to better themselves through smart real estate investing. Usually we don't know what we don't know. I don't have any children. I'm single. My parents are gone so I just hope to leave a legacy of someone who really cared. I know I cannot help everyone, but I hope to leave an indelible mark on as many people as I can just by being my true authentic self. Someone who cared.

Andy Wilkinson

Andy Wilkinson was born and raised in Homewood, Illinois, and moved to Flint, Michigan, to attend Kettering University (formerly GMI) five days after his eighteenth birthday. He received a Bachelor's degree in Mechanical Engineering in 2004. His education continued at Oakland University where he received a Master's degree in Mechanical Engineering in 2007. Currently he is attending Grand Canyon University in Phoenix, Arizona, pursing a Doctorate in Education (EdD) in Organizational Leadership.

His career began in 2000 as an engineering co-op student working for an automotive supplier. In his 16 years in the automotive industry, he flourished as an engineer and became a project chief engineer at Chrysler (FCA). After Chrysler, Andy went to an automotive supplier as a project manager and within six months he was promoted to team leader. In this position, he was the lead responsible for advanced research and development for North America.

He enjoyed working with mechanical systems, manufacturing processes, and problem solving but had some serious contentions with corporate America. In January 2017, he left his corporate job for the last time to pursue his dreams of creating his own business.

He purchased his first home in 2005, began investing in real estate in 2010, and has completed numerous transactions since. Now he is a business owner, real estate investor, and student. Andy believes in life-long learning and growth. His business plan is to educate and provide the framework for other like-minded individuals/entrepreneurs so they too can have the option of personal success and financial freedom without the corporate struggle many Americans contend with.

Contact information:
Email: ajw@cactusfinancialgroup.com
Website: www.cactusfinancialgroup.com

Shannon:
What inspired you to get into real estate?

Andy:
This is one of my favorite questions, especially for people that know my background. I lived the corporate America life for 16 long, long, years. Thankfully, I realized that was not the direction I wanted to go and much better options were available. During my career, I was fortunate to receive multiple raises, promotions, bonuses, and fancy job titles. However, I realized that it didn't matter how hard I worked, I still got the same measly paycheck every month. In addition, when you look at retirement, 401ks and stock options did not meet my expectations. Real estate really opened my mind as far as the amount of work you put into it is what you can get out of it, and no one can limit your paycheck.

Shannon:
Right.

Andy:
That's a big part of it and there are two distinct aspects of real estate that everyone may not fully understand. There are possibilities for short-term income, to live off, and potential to build long-

term wealth and passive income with rental properties and other various strategies. Having both income opportunities available, and not feeling trapped in what I considered a dead-end career, is really what turned me on to real estate.

Shannon:

Was there something that happened, because you know, I hear quite often, "I was in a job that was dead-end," or, "I was in a job that I was working my butt off, working 60-70 hours a week for little return, so I decided to switch the real estate." Well, I look at it as, what happened that made you decide real estate? Or did you meet somebody that made you decide real estate? Because 16 years ago, before you decided to be an engineer, real estate was there also, so what happened or who did you meet that made you decide real estate is the way to go?

Andy:

It was my own experience, right out of college; people would say, "go buy a house, it's the best asset you can ever buy." In 2005, the market was at its peak, and I was living in Michigan at the time, so I went out and got the 80-20 loan, an 80 percent mortgage with an adjustable interest rate and 20 percent on a line of credit. I had zero money to put down on it, so I basically swiped a credit card for 20 percent of my mortgage, and then I got duped into the adjustable rate mortgages which caused a lot of problems amongst the whole country. Perhaps a significant contributor to the whole financial crash in the 2008–2009 time frame.

I was honestly just upset from day one after I purchased that home. I saw the property value steadily decline year after year after everyone said, "this is the greatest asset you could ever buy." It turned out that was wrong. In 2008, I was working for an automotive supplier, and they were going through lay-offs because, as you know, the whole economy was in a downward spiral. I made it through six rounds of lay-offs; I've never been laid off or fired before, but I saw a lot of my friends, superiors, mentors get let go, like they were just a number, which, turns out, they were.

Shannon:

They were, yeah.

Andy:

Yeah, so that was really upsetting to me, so it's my personal experience. There wasn't anyone that said, "Hey, go do real estate." It was me living it and me learning that something was not right.

Shannon:

Perfect.

Andy:

My first intuition into something outside of the standard W2 world was while going through those lay-offs and with everybody getting axed, I assumed it was only a matter of time until my number was called. I picked up the *Rich Dad, Poor Dad* book by Robert Kiyosaki. I sat down and started reading and that's really what sparked my interest. I haven't put those types of books down since.

Shannon:

Nice, so how has your education in real estate changed the way that you invest, as opposed to your first home that you bought?

Andy:

It has 100 percent turned my vision around. In 2010, I went out and got a real estate license while I was still working full-time in engineering. I realized that I didn't want anything to do with showing other people houses. I'd help friends and family of course, but my interest was in analyzing the market and having access to the MLS and seeing what properties were selling at what values and things of that nature. I went out and bought a foreclosed property from the bank for $10,800. I saw it at midnight one night, with a flashlight. I was so excited that I went out and bought it the next day. Come to find out, the public records were incorrect. They said it was a single-family home, it turns out that it was a modular home with additions. I couldn't even tell during my "flashlight inspection." I ended up losing over $10,000 on that property. That was me before I became educated in real estate. Some people learn the hard way, and I'm an example of that.

Shannon:

Wow.

Andy:

Yeah.... So having the education and understanding what a good property is, you must know the ins and outs of it. You need to have experienced people to inspect the property and someone to appraise it. It's critical to understand what you›re really buying before you get into it.

Shannon:

What would you say is the number one mistake an individual makes when buying their first property? Would it be kind of what you just said, of having somebody that can come in and help appraise, or do you think that there's a bigger mistake that people make when buying their first property?

Andy:

Based on my experience, as I was guilty of this, it's rushing into the deal. I often hear people getting so excited about their first deal that they make the numbers work, or so they think. Everyone thinks the fix and flip game is so sexy because all the hype it gets on TV. Rookie investors often run out and jump right into their first deal, just so they can say they've done it, but they don't truly analyze it or understand what risks are involved. Simply including a safety factor as part of your deal, some people don't consider. A lot of starter investors make decisions based on emotions rather than based on the facts and numbers of the deal.

Shannon:

What's a safety factor?

Andy:

A safety factor is a term I learned that is commonly used in engineering, it accommodates for the unknown. Let's say you're going into a house, even if you have an appraiser and a home inspector go through the property, and you say, "okay, it's going to be $20,000 worth of renovation." In my business model, I'm going to put an extra 10 or maybe even 15 percent on top of that to account for the unknowns. When you start pulling apart walls, you find details you can't see with the naked eye. These are the details that you aren't aware of, that need to be fixed, and you don't know until you start into the project.

Shannon:

Got it. It's interesting that you said that not everybody builds a safety factor in because I'm not in real estate investing, but I know just from watching TV, just from watching all the fix and flip shows on HGTV, I always see unexpected costs come up on those. And you know, it's funny now that I'm saying this out loud, I don't think they necessarily build in extra costs or a safety factor on the TV shows.

Andy:

Definitely not, because...

Shannon:

Maybe that's just for TV.

Andy:

Yep, you nailed it right there. That's just for TV, it's entertainment.

Shannon:

That's probably true. If the TV shows don't teach you to do that, how did you learn? I mean, it sounds like you learned the hard way because you said you lost over $10,000 on your first property. Did you have a mentor that helped you, or did you read that in Rich Dad Poor Dad, or did you just learn from experience that, "Wow, I need to build in a safety factor"?

Andy:

Really, it was a combination of things. In all my engineering studies and in the real world, when designing parts we always built in a safety factor. After I had my mistake property in 2010 and lost a bunch of money, a little light went off in my head that said, wait a minute, let›s look at this. Use your knowledge, education and experience from other disciplines and apply it to real estate. Not only was it my big mistake, but it was just applying other resources that I've learned and other strategies that can be translated from engineering to real estate.

Shannon:

Got it. All right, so you bought your first house before the crash, and you bought your second mistake house after our economy crash. What would you say about the economy? Do you feel that real estate investing success is dependent on a strong economy?

Andy:

No, not at all; it depends on your strategy. An educated and experienced real estate investor will change their strategy and adapt to the market. If the economy is down and house prices are down, then that's a better opportunity for an investor to purchase and acquire properties at a discounted rate. Generally, when the economy is down, people don't have a lot of money to purchase new homes, so that would be an ideal time to do buy and holds and come up with lease options and rental properties. If the market is up, as it is now, it's a better time to do the fix and flips, where the retail prices are high and people also have money to purchase those homes, so now is an ideal time to sell properties at a retail price.

Shannon:

Great, so in a down economy, what is one of your favorite strategies for acquiring a home?

Andy:

My favorite process to acquire properties is 'subject to.' If somebody is having struggles with income and can't sell their property, you can acquire the property and leave it with the homeowner's current financing. Their mortgage would stay in place, and with the proper contract, you as the investor will now control the property and be responsible in making the mortgage payments. Next, you can move a new tenant in and generate cash flow based on the previous mortgage which was in place. It really makes an excellent deal when there is equity in the home. I think this is the most, what's a good word, I was going to say technologically advanced, but I think it's the most interesting way of acquiring property.

Shannon:

Great. Perfect. So what is one of your favorite strategies for acquiring homes in an up economy?

Andy:

Even in an up economy, there are still people that have issues with probates for example. If there is a death in the family, or if there are other issues and properties are vacant, a good deal may emerge. There are still people that lose their jobs and people looking for help, facing foreclosures. Homes in distressed areas you can acquire at a discounted rate, which turns those properties into a great candidate for a fix and flip or renovation. Since the economy is up, it's worth the investment to fix it and sell for retail value.

Shannon:

So, how do you find those homes? How do you know that a property is in distress or that somebody needs help?

Andy:

That's a great question. There are a couple creative ways to do it. You could do it through probate courts and by researching county records. Another fantastic way is through eviction courts. You can acquire property addresses and derive the owners contact information. Sometimes the owner acting as a landlord just wants to get out of the house which leaves an opportunity for a deal. There is also information available from title companies. You can find out if a property owner goes on a 60 or 90-day late or if they miss two or three payments on their mortgage; that triggers a notice of default which is public record. Then, you can find the address and go to the home and see if the people living there need help to move on.

Shannon:

You know, it's interesting. You are the first person I've spoken to in all the interviews I've done that talks about going to the court, to an eviction court. A few people have talked about probate, but explain to me, if somebody's in eviction court, so that means it's an active landlord.

Andy:
Correct.

Shannon:
That's kind of really cool. So let›s answer that question as you are doing it, because you›re about to. What I would like for you to do is kind of walk me through. How are you going to talk to that landlord? How are you going to get them to meet with you? How are you going to get them to know that you›re serious, and then what is the proposal that you are going to make? Are you going to use the 'subject to' type? Are you going to have time to do research on the homes before you get there? That possibly you could look at doing a short sale if the landlord wants out because they›ve taken out so many mortgages and they›re upside down? That›s a ton of information I just threw at you.

Andy:
Okay, well, let me give you a quick backdrop of why the courts turn me on.

Shannon:
Got you.

Andy:
My grandfather was a circuit court judge, back in Michigan, and my uncle is a lawyer and magistrate. My cousin is a lawyer, my mother is a paralegal, so we have a lot of law relations in my family. I've been raised seeing and hearing a lot of legal jargon and court-type discussions, which now that I think about it has had an influence. In addition, I've been through a few negative experiences throughout the court, but we'll save that story for another book. :)>

Shannon:
Okay.

Andy:

Being able to make profit while helping people through the court system is something I find extremely attractive. It's also something that I don't see very many people doing. My whole mantra is to be able to find leads that other people cannot find and do not find, so if something's on the MLS I'm generally not interested in it. I like to be more of a behind-the-scenes, private investigator kind of guy, so the court systems are of particular interest to me.

Shannon:

Can you find out the information on the house and the landlord information before court, or do you have to go to the court and basically walk up to people and say, "Hey, are you the property owner for this address?"

Andy:

Going to the court is more to get the addresses. You may get lucky to be there at the right time but it's hard to pick the owners to specific properties out of a crowd. I wouldn't be walking up to everyone and handing them my business card as they have an agenda. I'd be trying to find a list of properties or a list of names of the owners that are in the eviction court for that day.

Shannon:

Got it. Well that sounds actually super fun.

Andy:

I agree.

Shannon:

I am not even saying that facetiously. That sounds super fun to me. Now, probate court: do you think that you're going to handle probate court the same way, or do you think probate court is different than eviction court?

Andy:

It's a different scenario, a separate set of circumstances, but basically the same process. You're trying to find an address and the owners of a property in a distressed situation that are motivated to get out of that property. It doesn't really matter how you find it if you find someone that's in a situation where you can help them by getting them out of their property and they're motivated to do so. That's how you generate a high-quality property lead.

Shannon:

All right, well, while we're talking about this, I've also heard that tax liens you have to go down to the courts for. Do you plan on doing anything with tax liens?

Andy:

Absolutely. In the first quarter of every year is the best time to get into tax liens and deeds, depending on your state. That's a fantastic time to find properties where the owners owe taxes that have been delinquent. This is a clever way to acquire properties at a reduced rate. However, the turnaround is generally slow, so you don't get those properties right away. If your business model accommodates a certain amount of capital available in the first quarter of each year, then you could get in and put some offers on a few tax liens and deed deals. Then those are in the pipeline when they come to fruition over the next few months and you have more business opportunity.

Shannon:

All right. Let's look at fix and flip. When you're doing a fix and flip, what are the top three things that you want to look out for?

Andy:

For any property, finding the deal upfront is always my number one priority. I don't care if it's a fix and flip, a buy and hold, whatever your exit strategy is, finding the deal upfront is where you make your money. We always talk that you make your money when you purchase the house, then you get paid when you sell it. My number one strategy is always starting with the best possible deal.

Once you've done your analysis and found the deal, have a good inspector and experienced contractor walk the property with you.

Take note of every detail that needs to be fixed, accumulate all that information and add a safety factor. The next trick is not to overdo it. I've been caught in this before; with the engineering mindset I generally want to fix everything. If I find a problem, I want a solution; if it looks dirty, I want to clean it; if it looks broken, it›s got to be fixed. This is not a good strategy. You must look at the comps in the area. If none of the houses on your street or around your neighborhood have granite countertops, then your house does not need granite countertops. Same for windows, landscaping, and all other details that require money to upgrade.

Shannon:

What if they want granite countertops? What if you really want granite countertops?

Andy:

That's where you've got to set the emotion aside. For a fix and flip, it's not your house, so you have to remove the emotion from it. It truly doesn't matter what you want. It's what is right for that property, and what is good for that deal because it is a business. This isn't a property that you're going to move into.

Shannon:

Got it. Well, let's go back to your strategy. You're looking at buy and holds, is that correct?

Andy:

My favorite strategy is wholesaling right now, due to the market, but depending on what the deal is, buy and holds are my second favorite.

Shannon:

The properties that you're looking to get from the eviction court, you're looking at wholesaling those?

Andy:
Correct.

Shannon:

All right, so here's my question. Do you have a specific type of home, so if you go down to the eviction court and every single home that is in the eviction court that day is a two-bedrooms one-bathroom, are you interested in two-bedroom one-bathrooms, or would that be a day that you go, "Oh, today was a bad day," and you go home?

Andy:

If there is a plethora of two-bedrooms one-bathrooms, I will not close my eyes to that. My target market is what we call a starter home plus one, so I prefer a three-bed two-bath; I'll deal with a three bed one bath if it's a good deal. The other thing about staying within that range is you learn to do quick math. Based on the numbers and the zip code, you can quickly calculate price per square foot, which gives a fast estimate of the deal. It's like when you go grocery shopping and you see the same things that you buy all the time and you understand what's a deal and what's not. If there's a good deal then you know you want to buy 20 of them because it's a great deal right now, so it's like that where you really start to understand the market but you've got to start by focusing on one style of property, in a specific area.

Shannon:

You know, I loved it especially when you talked about comparing it to grocery shopping. I love that you brought up the price per square foot because so many people say, "Well, it's a three-two for $100,000—that's a great deal." Well, there are three-twos that are 1200 square feet, and there are three-twos that are 2000 square feet, so it's like that box of cereal when it's two for five and everyone goes, "Well, that's a great deal." Well, no it's not. That's still 30 cents per ounce, as opposed to 7 cents per ounce.

Andy:

Exactly.

Shannon:

I actually laughed a little inside when you compared it to grocery shopping, so good job! All humans can relate to that! Okay, real estate and massive income and passive income. Wholesaling is all about creating massive income. You find a property, you acquire it, you get it under contract, and then you make money right then and there.

Andy:
Yes.

Shannon:
If you decide to stop wholesaling tomorrow, do you have passive income? Is there a way to create that with wholesaling?

Andy:
Wholesaling is to generate short-term income, not passive. My business model consists of wholesales plus periodic fix and flips for short-term income while building a small nest egg. When I acquire enough cash, and using other strategies like 'subject to,' I will continue purchasing buy and holds. Wholesaling is the fastest, most efficient way to generate income through real estate. Acquiring rental properties is how to generate passive income and long-term wealth. I want to mention a quote from Warren Buffett regarding passive income that really struck me. He says, "if you don't learn how to make money while you sleep, you'll work until you die."

Shannon:
That really hits home.

Andy:
Yes, I agree 100 percent, and I believe it wholeheartedly.

Shannon:
As you are building up your wholesaling profile, how do you make sure that you're going to be able to wholesale that home? What happens if you get it under contract and you don't find a buyer? How do you make sure that you have buyers lined up?

Andy:

That's an excellent question. I'll tell you two different sides of that coin. Part of that is working with a community and a team of investors; so here in Phoenix, we have three groups locally in the valley that are active in real estate. I'm connected with all three groups. Once your name gets out there as a credible, experienced wholesaler, then the buyers will start coming to you, and they'll be waiting on you to find properties.

The other side of it is, when you get the property under contract you always have an exit strategy, so if for some reason you cannot find a buyer or another issue arises, you can leave it subject to an inspection, for example, and have an out.

Shannon:

You were talking about getting your name out there in the wholesale. Why would an investor use a middle-man? Why wouldn't they just go find that property themselves?

Andy:

As I mentioned before, you don't see or hear very many people talking about going to the eviction courts, probate courts, or doing the actual investigation for pre-foreclosures and the behind the scenes work of finding these properties. Sure, an investor can go out and buy a property off the MLS any day; you can pick up the phone, call a realtor, and buy a property, but are they really going to make a true profit on that, considering the risks? My answer is, I doubt it. My business model optimizes each deal.

Shannon:

Let's talk about cash flow. What is cash flow, and why is it such an important focus of your business?

Andy:

Absolutely. Cash flow is the focal point of my business and should be of anyone's business. Cash flow is simply your income minus your expenses, and I think a lot of people don't accommodate for all expenses. I have a couple rental properties right now, and before I got educated and started working with other experienced investors, I didn't accommodate for certain things and turns out I wasn't making as much money as I thought. Cash flow is what makes your bank account either rise or fall. That's 100 percent critical for any business.

Shannon:

All right, so you own a couple rental properties right now. Do you have a favorite rental property?

Andy:

I have a favorite rental property because it's my first home I purchased in 2005 that I was too stubborn to get rid of. I was always underwater with it, and I still have that property rented out today. I'm kind of proud of that because I've turned what was a financial nightmare into a profitable deal.

Shannon:

I'm so proud of you for that.

Andy:

Thank you.

Shannon:

Okay, tell me the story about rental properties. Tell me, so you bought it in 2005. You were upside down for a while. Tell me how you got into the upside-down situation and how you have turned it around today.

Andy:

Okay, I bought the property in 2005 for $173,000, and it's a little three-bed two-bath tri-level in beautiful Lake Orion, Michigan, on a treacherous dirt road. But, it backs up to the Bald Mountain recreational area, which is great for mountain biking, hiking, and fishing. I feel like I'm giving a sales pitch.

Shannon:

That's what I felt like as I was reading it right now on the MLS.

Andy:

lived in the property for about five years and re-did every room but the basement. I put in nice tile floors, fancy countertops, of course a lot higher end than it needed to be and a lot more expensive than that neighborhood required. I realized that the money I'd put into it I wouldn't get out for a long time. Renting it out was my only real option. I rented it out in 2010, and the tenants are still in the property today. I worked out a good deal and the house was in great shape, as it was basically brand-new on the inside.

Shannon:

Now, do you think you'll ever sell that home? Would you ever put that under a lease option contract with them?

Andy:

I've tried to do a lease option with them, but they weren't interested in purchasing it. The father is an elementary school teacher, he's a great guy but doesn't make a ton of income, and the wife is a stay-at-home mom. As of late she's been working some part-time jobs because they're late on their water bill. I don't penalize them because they always pay. They're usually a week or two late, but they've always paid for the last seven years now, and I understand their situation. At the end of the day it's all about helping people, so insignificant details and circumstances don't bother me as long as they are good, genuine, hardworking people.

I never refinanced the house. I paid off the 20 percent the line of credit but still have an adjustable rate mortgage, which has been under 4 percent for the last 7 or 8 years. Since the interest rates were so low, it never made sense to refinance it.

Shannon:

Right.

Andy:

Now that the interest rates are starting to rise and rumors exist they will continue to rise, I have inquired about refinancing, but that resets the amortization schedule, which I have a problem with. With our latest lease extension, they plan on moving out next April, so this would be a great exit for me. If they move out in April, I don't have to acquire the closing costs associated with refinancing. I don't have to reset the amortization schedule for refinancing the loan. I'll get it fixed up and on the market in May, which is a fantastic time to sell. To answer your question, long-winded, yes, I do plan on selling it the middle of next year.

Shannon:
With your 80/20 it sounds like you have good equity in that home. Did that economy bounce back?

Andy:
Yes, so I did inquire about refinancing recently. The value they used for the refinance calculation was $180,000 and I owe just over $100,000, so I do have equity in that home.

Shannon:
Why would you not plan on just holding onto that home and keeping it as a rental? Is it because you now live in Phoenix, and it's too hard to manage from that far away?

Andy:
That's part of it. However, I do have a property manager for the homes I own in Michigan. My real motivation is to save about $3500 in closing costs to refinance, plus it would reset the amortization schedule, which just bothers me. I would sell as the market is up and put that equity towards another property or perhaps two.

Shannon:
Right.

Andy:
I'll re-evaluate this next year when the time comes, but right now, it doesn't make sense to refinance at a higher interest rate, reset the amortization schedule, and pay the closing costs.

Shannon:

Got it, okay, so you have to either refinance your ARM or sell.

Andy:

Correct.

Shannon:

Got it. Okay. Now I'm coming full circle. It's not an option anymore to not refinance.

Andy:

Right. It wouldn't make sense to let the interest rate keep rising.

Shannon:

Okay, perfect. So when you sell that home, do you think you'll continue to invest in Michigan, or do you think that you will start investing more in Phoenix?

Andy:

My thought right now is, based on the way the market is, that I will do my wholesaling and some fix and flips locally here in Phoenix. I do know some wonderful places in Michigan that I plan to continue my buy and hold strategy and utilize my established real estate network.

Shannon:

What is the legacy that you would like to leave behind?

Andy:

The legacy for me is extremely important and truly what it is all about. My 16 years in corporate America I consider "doing time." I was unhappy and felt trapped which became very depressing. I want to be an example and show everyone there are better options outside corporate America. There are too many people who simply accept being un-happy with their jobs and daily lives. In addition to leaving a strong financial portfolio for my family, I want to inspire people to find happiness in what they do. My grandfather said, "if you love what you do, you'll never work a day in your life." As a business owner, entrepreneur, doctoral student, husband, and father, I have never been busier in my life but also have never been this happy. If you are not happy, I challenge you to evaluate what you want in this life. Whether it's in real estate or creating your own business, you must take the first step. Get educated, surround yourself with like-minded people, and don't stop until your dreams come true.

Dominic Wood

Dominic Wood is a real estate broker, investor, property manager and RE trainer in Seattle, Washington. He began a career in real estate in 2006 with experience in both residential and commercial properties. Mr. Wood has worked with developers in building new construction town-homes and apartment buildings and providing project management, interior design, property leasing, and maintenance support.

Dominic became a partner at Vis A Vis Real Estate Co. in 2016, managing the greater Seattle sales team. His team specializes in raising capital, flipping homes, listing million+ dollar properties, apartment buildings, and new development projects in and around Seattle.

Dominic is also a team leader of the RISE Seattle Renatus Team and the Legacy Real Estate Investment Team. His team hosts investor workshops, fix & flip property tours, and weekly study group sessions training students how to become real estate investors.

Contact Info:
Dominic welcomes questions at Domwood@gmail.com or visit his website at www.LegacyREITeam.com for more info.

Shannon:

I know that you are in real estate investing. What inspired you to get into real estate?

Dominic:

I was introduced to real estate at age 26. I had recently graduated college with a degree in Marketing and was pursuing a career in Advertising. That was my passion: sales, marketing, and advertising. I got a call from my brother-in-law, Cole Hatter, a young and energetic entrepreneur from Orange County. He had recently been in recovery from some traumatic accidents, losing two of his best friends, and I was eager to hear how he was doing. He had flown up from California and said, "Dominic, you need to learn about real estate." His life had completely turned around for the better, and he had a renewed purpose in life, helping others gain financial literacy, and I was fascinated by seeing what could capture his interest so well. His focus on real estate and becoming an entrepreneur was exciting and I said, "If this guy can do it, so can I." Of course, at the time, I had just finished college, and I thought I had found my career. After spending an evening with Cole at a real estate investor workshop, I was instantly bitten by the real estate bug. The real estate market was booming at the time and it absolutely blew me away. I had no previous concept of real estate investing. I had no idea about using leverage to buy properties and build equity. I had no idea about wealth planning for the long term. It immediately intrigued yet shocked me that I had just spent nearly $100K and 4.5 years in college and hadn't learned anything about financial literacy, about banking, or about investing in real estate, some of the most important investments we can ever make. I didn't even know how a mortgage works. I didn't know anything about how our economy is massively influenced by the real estate market. I did realize how much I didn't know, and I wanted to learn more. So, I signed up with his team and it began of path of exploration, networking, and non-stop education from some of the most successful real estate investors in the world.

As eager as I was to start investing in real estate, it took some time to get educated. This is not a get rich quick industry, but I was being trained by some of the most wealthy investors in the world. I had to start from the basics, and that's what I did. I focused on entrepreneur necessities like setting up entities, tax deductions, and real estate essentials. I was very lucky to be introduced to experts who were willing to give their time to teach me. It was worth every penny to invest in my real estate education.

I spent several years learning about various creative investment strategies and eventually I got to the point where I had the confidence to start pulling the trigger, building a business, starting to work in the foreclosure market doing short sales, and going to the auctions and meeting investors—and confidently having conversations about investing in real estate with other experts.

Shannon:
Did you attempt to do any investing before you got educated? Were you bit by the bug and thought, "I'm going to jump into this"?

Dominic:
No, I had no background at all. I had nothing. My family didn't invest in real estate besides our own personal residence. I had a uncle who had four rental houses. That was the extent. It just wasn't in our family or in our business. It just wasn't something that we did, so it was all new to me. But my parents have come around and currently invest in my real estate projects and are actively looking at rental properties, building their own portfolios. As for attempting to invest before being educated, I see it almost every day, people who get themselves upside down, trying to figure it out the hard way. Investors will learn one way or the other, but I have never lost money on a deal because we know what we're doing.

Shannon:
In all of your education and all of the learning that you've been doing, what is one of the top real estate strategies that you have learned about that you really enjoy using?

Dominic:
I would say that there's two strategies that we mainly utilize right now: wholesaling and fixing and flipping real estate. Wholesaling

has been an incredible strategy. That's what I really enjoy doing because you don't need any money to do it. I partnered up with some experienced and successful investors who helped me get started. They were very well-educated, and they said, "Hey, here's how you talk to a potential motivated seller... Here are some leads... Just follow the plan. Go out and ask these homeowners if they're open to selling their houses." I did that on a daily basis. I would just go out and knock on doors and have a contract in hand, and say "Hey, my name's Dominic. I'm interested in buying some houses in your area. Are you interested in selling?" Every 'No' leads to an eventual 'Yes.' Any sales business will have similar rejections and once you get past the fear of being rejected, you realize every 'No' will eventually lead to a 'Yes, I want to sell.' I've since then decided to build a team of sales associates, property analysts, and I have built a team of investors to assist with acquiring our deals. My job now is to make the offers that my sales team finds, and we can decide if we want to keep them for our own flips or wholesale them to other investors.

Shannon:

How did your first wholesale deal come about?

Dominic:

It took about 30–45 days before my first deal came to me from door knocking. The woman said, "Yeah, I'm looking at selling the house." Her mother had passed away, the home was in foreclosure, and she had nearly $60K in medical liens. She was about to lose everything. I put the property under contract and we were able to negotiate a settlement with the lien holders so she could make around $55K, and we then sold the contract to purchase to another investor who was going to then fix it and flip it and that investor paid us $25,000. It took less than four weeks and it was a total WIN-WIN-WIN situation for everyone. What other industry can you make $25,000 in one month on one sale, save a woman's inheritance so she can afford to move into a nice apartment, and walk away knowing if we hadn't helped her she would have lost it all? Every deal is a process in negotiation, but they tend to be very lucrative. I've wholesaled properties for up to $60,000 in less than 4 weeks. That's insane. It's better than most real estate brokers make on a normal commission. And it's so much more money than I was making in advertising or my previous jobs. After some experience in wholesaling properties, we now require a list back on our deals, so we will re-list the properties after an investor remodels the house and make another commission on the back end. Boom, another WIN!

Shannon:
What other types of real estate have you done?

Dominic:
Since I started learning to invest in real estate in 2006, I have attempted all sorts of investing strategies. I've attempted managing short sales. Those are very complicated. You have to be very experienced and the laws have changed quite a bit in Washington state, so that's not the easiest thing to do anymore and not my preference.

I had attempted brokering commercial real estate, and I worked for a commercial brokerage for a couple of years from 2008-2010. That's about when the market crashed and we watched it all happen in real time as we were monitoring the CMBS market closely, and we couldn't get any deals closed because the banks wouldn't approve our sales. The market crash took our small brokerage down, and I was so disappointed. I had spent years investing time and money into the industry and looked around at a collapsed market. I took some big licks when everything was crashing, even though I knew that real estate was such a good industry to be in, but it was a very challenging time to be in it. So, I took a break from the business for a small period of time. I had an opportunity join a restaurant partnership and had a great time, but I knew I would go back to real estate eventually. I did some new construction project management with another buddy who was building homes, so that I could stay involved in the field, but I wasn't investing myself. I had the opportunity to work with a developer who had multi-family properties and they hired me as their property manager. It was a valuable experience and it kept me going financially.

It wasn't until I eventually cut ties with everyone that I had been working for and said, "I need to go out and do this for myself." And that's when I found my current business partner. Rob Knoles was my original business partner; we had started learning together in 2006 after I helped introduce him to the same education team Cole had introduced me to. He focused on a different strategy from me and learned how to fix up old houses and did very well focusing on his niche for over ten years, flipping hundreds of homes. I think it's important to remember that we all have our own paths, so while I observed his successes from a distance, I was building my own skills. Rob learned to manage fix & flips and built a small real estate brokerage. We have since built an office, a team of sales associates, a team of project managers, we've raised millions in capital and it's been an incredible opportunity to work with my best friend over the last couple years.

Shannon:

How do you think all of that experience has helped you in the way that you invest in real estate now?

Dominic:

I think it all came full circle back in 2015, I had sold the restaurant, and I called my buddy Rob, and I said, "All right, I want to fix and flip houses." I never actually had done that but he had done it for ten years. For one, you have to be ready to for dealing with big numbers, getting comfortable dealing with hundreds of thousands of dollars. You have to communicate effectively with people. Working in a restaurant, working in property management, and working in sales, that was very beneficial to me in addition to my education. I was able to at least come to the table being comfortable with talking to people even if I was nervous jumping back into the biz. From there I just needed a little bit of direction from someone who was experienced in buying hundreds of homes and raising capital. Rob had a lot of experience fixing and flipping and buying wholesale properties. Once I partnered with him, he just gave me a little bit of a direction and said, "You can do this." That's really all I needed.

From there, I found my place, and I took on the role of managing acquisitions, managing our investor partners, and then bringing other people into our team because I had quite a bit of management experience. I realized that I could bring other people into our business who could do what I was doing. If I could get five, six, seven other people out there knocking on doors and setting the appointments for us, I can sit down with those sellers and negotiate to buy their houses all day long.

Shannon:

How far into you starting to do your real estate investing did you realize how important it was to have a team that was established?

Dominic:

I know I certainly couldn't be where I am today unless I had started with a team that was experienced. We currently mentor quite a few novice investors, people who have never purchased a house or people who have never even talked to a home owner about selling their house. The most important thing that we say is "Go get educated" because I don't teach people how to invest in real estate but I know an organization that does. Join us at Renatus and we will teach you how to invest in real estate and once you know how to do it, then we're going to give you that additional guidance to actually going out and doing it.

That's what I needed because I knew how to do it. I just hadn't done it. Once I had that additional hand holding to get through my first deal, and my second deal, that's all I needed. I just went from like 5 miles an hour to 100 miles an hour within just the last year, buying and selling over $12 million in real estate while building an awesome team that's out there crushing it. Once they got their first deal done, they're speeding up and they're doing more deals. It's really accelerated our business by tapping into a network of real estate investors who are educated and who just need a little bit of guidance.

Shannon:

Right. How do you think your mentors in real estate investing helped you navigate potential pitfalls and how do you make sure that you help the people you're mentoring?

Dominic:

Well, one thing that I can say about my current business partners and mentors is they've flipped hundreds of houses, bought and sold hundreds of houses, so I'm very lucky I work with very experienced investors. It's not by chance though. I reached out to them. It's not by chance that I went to the people that I know have years of real estate investing education. I purposely went to them. So how have they helped? I ask a lot of questions. If I don't know the answer, I don't try to make it up. I don't freeze up and quit. I can go back to my education. If I need questions answered, I can go to my investor coaches. I can go to my business partners. I can go to any one of my team members that are involved in our title or escrow, our investor capital hard money lenders, our other business associates, our real estate attorney. It's all about surrounding yourself with people smarter than you. And perhaps I had to fake it till I made it, stumble thru until I knew what I was doing. But I never stop learning and I'm always looking for more people that I can tap into.

Shannon:

Give me a real life example. Give me an example of where you thought, "You know, I'm going to try this. Let me run it by one of my mentors and see what they say." It can be a positive or a negative. It can be where they came back and they're like, "Oh my gosh. Yeah. That was brilliant. That's exactly how you do it." Or it can be where they saved your rear on something.

Dominic:

One of the most complex strategies that is out there is buying a property 'subject to' the existing loan. Buying the property with an existing loan from a home owner seems crazy, but someone who is in a situation where they need to get out of their home before they get foreclosed on and they really have little equity left, where we can provide a solution for them, this is something that had long intrigued me, but I had never done it until we came across a small 2BR condo in North Seattle. The condo was in foreclosure. The homeowner owed about $97,000 in loans and HOA dues. He had about a $57,000 first, a $27,000 second, and a $13,000 HOA in arrears. So a total of around $97,000. By our calculations, the condo really just needed about $20,000 in repairs, and we could resell it for $175,000. It's a small deal relative to the majority of our projects, but I saw the opportunity, and we knew that we could help this seller out. We didn't really need to get a loan for this particular deal. We could just buy the property subject to his existing loans, so he was willing to sign with us that we would pay him $10,000 cash for his condo, and then he would essentially agree to sign a contract that he would stay liable for his $57,000 loan, and stay liable for his $27,000 loan, and we would just make the payments. Then, he also had a $13,000 HOA bill in arrears. I was able to purchase his condo essentially by just paying off the HOA, and his $10,000 cash, so we essentially bought his condo for around $27,000 with the closing fees. We put $20,000 into the remodel, so we're into it for roughly around $50,000 with fees. We then flipped it and put it back on the market for $175,000 and sold it all cash with a 3 week closing for over asking at $188,888. Nearly $45,000 profit in less than 60 days! But the cool thing about this was we didn't use any loans. We raised the $50,000 to do the deal from one of our investor partner's IRA accounts for 15 percent annual Interest, so I had no money of my own in the deal.

The challenge that came up was I had never done this before. I called Gavin McCaleb, one of my mentors and asked him to help me with the proper contracts to pull off the deal. Being a part of an investor network like Renatus, all our contracts and forms are readily available, so I then ran it by an attorney. My attorney reviewed the docs; he said, "Yeah, this form looks great. Let's just add a couple items here and there that the seller needs to initial that he understands what he's signing." Once I was completed with that, we had bought the condo. We closed. He got his $10,000 and was able to move on. We paid the HOA. The condo was remodeled within 30 days, and back on the market. The banks were happy because they were going to get paid. The homeowner was happy. The HOA was happy they got paid. We made $45,000 profit. Everything falls into place when you're able to find creative solutions.

Shannon:

Was this one of your first deals?

Dominic:

This was my first 'subject to' deal, which made it complicated. A 'subject to' deal is not a simple deal process because you're not paying off the loan, and that can bring up a lot of issues for some lenders. Some people might say, 'but that's going to violate the due on sale clause,' and yes it does, but we work with the lenders to satisfy their needs, which is to get paid based on the current loan terms and once they get their money, that due on sale clause doesn't seem like such a big deal anymore. In this situation, we just notified them of what we were doing and told them that they would be paid within 45 to 60 days. One of them said, "Great, we're happy to do that. Thanks for telling us."

Shannon:

What do you like about doing a 'subject to'? What do you dislike?

Dominic:

I have not done one since then. It's something that I would certainly do again, though. I would actually consider changing the strategy from buying the property 'subject to,' to probably doing more of a lease option. With the lease option, we wouldn't have had to close on the property. We could have just had the option to buy and then assign that lease option to a new buyer at a later point. That would have probably saved us some money on excise tax fees and it would have kept everything in the exact same situation. So, I did learn some things from that process where I may adjust my strategy for a similar outcome.

Shannon:

That's nice that you have that option to adjust your strategy because not everybody would necessarily have that option. With that being said, what other strategies have you used to purchase or acquire properties?

Dominic:

Another strategy that we've recently completed was a short sale.

Short sales are not as common in Seattle as they used to be, mainly because property values are going up so much, but there's still people upside down on their loans. We found a house up in North Seattle. The homeowner, Tom, had moved out and he had left the state. Tom now lives in Texas, so we had to track him down. He said, "Well, what do I want to do with this property? It's upside down. I don't care about it. Do whatever you want."

We said, "Okay, here's our plan. It's upside down. We want to negotiate with the bank to get a discount on it." He signed the contract to allow us to do that. In this situation what we learned was we can hire a team of short sale experts to manage the short sale, so we paid a 1 percent commission to them from the purchase price to manage our short sale. The short sale negotiation is a complex process, so I am more than happy to delegate as many tasks as I can. Again, another important reason to have good people on your team is that you know what they're doing.

We were able to negotiate and purchase that house. We had initially made the offer for $190,000 and the bank came back with a counter offer at $210,000. We settled on $210,000 and then invested about $50,000 into it. We partnered with an investor who used his retirement plan to fund the project, so I had no money out of pocket in the deal and we then listed and sold the property for $340,000 making a $50,000 profit. It took about five months to do this project from initial negotiation with seller and lender to the remodel and resale.

Shannon:
You keep talking about how strong the real estate economy or the real estate market is in Seattle. Do you feel like real estate investing is dependent on a strong market or strong economy?

Dominic:
No. I don't. I think there's certainly cycles to real estate values. I know that Seattle is definitely in a bit of a bubble, but we have a lot more to go as far as property value increases in this area. There's just such a high demand for various industries here, and Seattle has been named the #1 real estate market for the last couple years because people are moving here in droves.

Our strong industry is driving up our property values. That can't last forever, but if something were to happen, we are very well-positioned to purchase properties when the property values are down, or if something happened with the economy we're very well-positioned because we know how to buy properties in foreclosure. We know how to buy properties that are upside down, that are short sales. Whether the market's going up or down, we still have opportunities to buy at either a discount or utilizing a creative strategy where we aren't using our cash or credit. We know how to buy them low no matter what the market is doing.

Shannon:

Okay. You actually just led right into my next question, so how do you feel that learning multiple investing strategies protects you and accelerates your investing success?

Dominic:

I look at my real estate education as building a tool belt. Whenever a deal comes across my desk that's going to require some kind of creative strategy, whether it's a short sale, or a 'subject to,' or a lease option, or an equity sharing situation, I have to be able to pull out a tool from my creative strategy investor tool belt, to be able to make that deal go through. We work in a market where we're not buying properties that are typically free and clear on title or ready to move-in like an MLS retail listed property. You have to know every strategy in order to know what to do when you come across a complex opportunity. I know investors come across deals everyday and often times don't know what to do and may walk away from a ton of potential profit.

Shannon:

Right. Do you think that one of the reasons that people fail at real estate is they don't know enough strategies? By strategies I mean, either to enter a property or to exit a property?

Dominic:

Yeah. Absolutely. I see it all the time. We see investors buy properties that they've paid way too much for. We see investors who buy properties that they might have bought the property at the right price, and then they put too much into the rehab. They went over budget because they didn't know what they were doing as far as remodeling goes or managing contractors. Those are the two main things. If you buy the property too high, you really didn't know what you were doing. You're going to have a challenge reselling it and making a profit. If you went over your budget, or the budget that should have been for that deal, that cuts into your profit as well. You have to be able to budget your deals properly, and you have to know when to say no if a seller won't lower their price or you need to renegotiate the terms, where you can pay their price but at a later time after you resell the property.

Shannon:
What is the number one thing that you want to look out for when you are doing a fix and flip?

Dominic:
Because of the market we are in, I will oftentimes put a property under contract without ever even seeing the house. That doesn't mean we buy it, but we may need to get it under contract to control the deal. What I have to be able to do is first and foremost is calculate the After Repair Value of the house. That has to be solid. You cannot fudge your ARV. You have to know what you're going to sell that property for and what the market's willing to pay. If you have that number wrong and you went through your whole project and you can't sell your house for the number that you thought you were going to sell it for, you're going to be completely upside down or not make a profit at all. That's the number one thing that I start with: what is this property going to be valued at.

Secondly is when we go in and we do our rehab estimate. That's where my business partner, Rob, comes in. He's in charge of construction. He manages all of our projects, but he's the expert at estimating repairs. An investor should always start off working with a contractor who is the expert and knows how to budget for a remodel. What we train our sales associates to do is go through a full, detailed checklist of the property condition from roof, to siding, to interior, to landscaping, to kitchens, baths, floors, walls, paint, etc. Everything needs to be checked off and budgeted accordingly: what needs to be fixed, what can stay, etc. Once that budget's in line, that's when I then can analyze and calculate my purchase price. Without an accurate After Repair Value, and without that budget for that construction, then there's no way you can have an accurate purchase price.

From there, you can work with a price range for your purchase price. You might be able to adjust some remodel costs, perhaps change some of your materials or change some of your design plans if you possibly have to purchase your property for a little bit higher than you initially budget for, so understanding what's adjustable is key.

Once I have the budget and the ARV, I do the property analysis using a pro-forma calculation based on purchase options. How will we purchase this? All cash? Using hard money? Do we need a construction loan? There's several variables and options, but we take them all into account to determine the best ROI. Once I come up with a purchase number that will fit our ROI requirements, I can then go into negotiation mode with the seller. I lay it all out for them. I just say, "This is our budget. This is what needs to be done with your house. Do you agree?" Often times they will agree. I walked the house with them, but I say to them, "It's either you do this work and you put the money in and you spend the six months getting your house to this condition so that you can sell it for this much, or you can just sell it to me right now, no conditions, all cash, close within 21 days. You can be rid of the situation today." That's usually how I approach it.

Shannon:

You said, "Of course, they agree because I walked the house with them." Have you ever had somebody not agree?

Dominic:

Yes, of course. Oftentimes, the homeowner, especially in a market like ours, wants more because the market's so crazy. They may say, "Well, my neighbor sold a house for $500,000, or $50,000, more than you're offering right now." A lot of times they will have done their own research on Zillow, and we may need to renegotiate or we'll have to justify my numbers further. Sometimes it's something in between, but I always want to make it a win-win situation. And if it doesn't work, then we can walk away or we can list the house for a retail price and make a 3 percent commission. Either way, we will have a solution for the homeowner. Oftentimes though, we are talking with people whose homes are in very rough shape and they will see the benefit of selling to us for cash vs. trying to sell on the retail market.

Shannon:

You said that you are at the point now where you're buying some of your homes unseen. As you're talking about having all of these budgets and how you're walking through with the homeowner, if you're buying a home unseen, how do you navigate those pitfalls? How do you navigate if you have an untruth? What if the homeowner sent you a picture of the yard and that picture of the yard is a year old, so what they sent you was their brand new sod and all their new shrubbery when actually they already ripped all that out and sold it because they were in a desperate market? How do you prepare for a situation like that?

Dominic:

When I say I buy houses that I haven't seen, it doesn't mean that none of my team members hasn't seen it. Someone has seen the house on my team, but there are many properties that I'll put the whole deal together and I haven't even walked it myself yet. That's just having the confidence in my team's abilities to do a deal. We don't rely on anyone else besides our direct team members to walk a deal. It can't just be the homeowner or a broker. A broker or homeowner may tell us what a property's value is or what repairs need to be done, but everything has to be verified by myself and my business partners in order for a deal to go through. But it says a lot about my team, that I have enough trust in my business partners that I will go through a purchase of a property without having seen it.

Shannon:

You're investing is all in Seattle. Have you thought about going into other markets that are maybe not as strong of a real estate market as Seattle?

Dominic:

Yes, absolutely. I think one of the benefits about Seattle is you can fix and flip real estate here and make a ton of money. You can make $50,000 to $100,000 and more, much more on a single deal. We had a property that sold for $300,000 profit last year. I've seen investors make $400,000 on new development projects. You can make a ton of money fixing and flipping and wholesaling deals, but the property values are so high that it's nearly impossible to buy and hold a cash flow investment in Seattle. So, in the terms of investing outside of our market, that's the next step for our business. We've talked about it quite a bit internally, finding the best markets for investing into buy and holds and building a portfolio outside of Seattle. It might be in south Seattle, like the Tacoma area. It might be very far north in Bellingham or it might be in eastern Washington where property values are a quarter or a third of Seattle property values but the rental market and rental income are still strong. That's the reason why we would need to look in these other areas away from the major metro market. We are also considering other states such as Ohio, Illinois, and Indiana as the purchase amounts can be as low as $20,000, which is incredible.

Shannon:

Tell me why would you want to have buy and hold properties in your portfolio?

Dominic:

A buy and hold strategy may typically start out with buying one or two houses; maybe you buy one house a year for the next five years. It could be just a starter house for some college kids. It could be a rental house for a small family. Essentially the goal is to buy a rental home where someone is paying your mortgage payment and they're giving you enough money from the rent minus expenses where you can put a couple hundred dollars in your pocket. Now your first house probably isn't going to make you rich, but there's a ton of benefits by having a rental property. You get tax deductions from your mortgage interest. You get a tax deduction from the depreciation of the property, while at the same time the property value is actually increasing in equity. So, while you're taking tax deductions, you're actually increasing your net worth from the property appreciation.

Shannon:

You've got the tax deduction from owning the home, but you have an increase in your net worth. How does that work? How do you get the tax deduction from owning the home, yet you have an increase in your net worth?

Dominic:

A house can depreciate. Right after you purchase the house you can start taking depreciation deductions of the purchase price for 27 and a half years, where you can depreciate the value of the property, so every year you're reducing your tax liabilities. Plus, if there's any costs for repairs, you can deduct those expenses as well. The most important thing is that you're getting an increase in appreciation, which relative to the stock market and any other investments long term, real estate always appreciates. It never really goes down. Yes, there's fluctuations, but it always increases over time. If you hold a real estate property for long term, you will be able to sell it for more than you bought it for. That's your net worth.

This also becomes very useful for when you want to borrow against your equity, or the value of your house minus what you still owe; you can do this and invest in more real estate. It's a piggy bank for you. You can use this as your retirement. You could borrow against your property using a HELOC, or a line of credit, and that could actually be used to pay down your mortgage payments allowing you to payoff your 30-year mortgage much faster and avoid paying a ton in interest. It doesn't take very many properties that you've purchased to start having large lines of credit that you can start buying more and more properties. It just becomes a snowball effect for your investment portfolio once you have just a couple of properties under your belt and enough appreciation, you really don't need any more cash or capital beyond just the equity that you have in your properties to build an awesome real estate investment portfolio. That's a huge benefit to buying and holding.

Shannon:

Most millionaires and billionaires have investments in commercial real estate. Why do you think commercial real estate is a good investment?

Dominic:

I did work for a commercial real estate brokerage for a while called Clearview Real Estate Capital in Issaquah, Washington, and I know that through my experience working with clients there as well as some of my current clients who own and operate commercial real estate buildings and businesses through those buildings that they are just on a whole other level of real estate investing. It certainly takes a lot of experience, a lot of education, and It doesn't have to be your own capital, but it certainly has to be a large amount of capital to be able to put some large commercial deals together.

Shannon:

It's a whole different animal, but do you see yourself wanting to get into that market? Or do you think you'll just want to stick with residential?

Dominic:

Yes, it's definitely something I'd like to do convert over to in the future from residential to commercial. I don't think I have an intention of keeping and maintaining residential buildings for super long, having been a property manager for multiple apartment buildings. I have no desire to manage tenants. I will do it, mainly because of the passive income, but I also do lease commercial buildings, and it's so much easier to deal with commercial tenants than it is to deal with residential tenants because if they're in business, typically they will respect the building. They'll respect the space that they're leasing, and as business owners they take care of themselves and they take care of the office space. Usually you don't have to worry about too much, whereas with rental tenants you have all sorts of headaches. I can certain see why commercial real estate investors would stick with that.

Shannon:

What type of legacy do you want to leave?

Dominic:

I initially got started investing in real estate because I saw the financial potential it could give me. But over the years, my purpose has changed, for one important reason. And that's because I made the decision to adopt my niece and take on the biggest challenge of my life. But now that I'm raising a little girl and I enjoy all sorts of outdoor activities, I think having a 9 to 5 job sounds awful. I like to sleep in, I like to hit the gym or go snowboarding during the week, I like being able to take Ashlyn with me to all sorts of trips and sporting activities. If I had a regular job, I would never be able to have the time freedom, nor could I probably afford to do all the fun things we get to do. I knew that my investing education was incredibly valuable, and I wanted to put it to use. I wanted to really be able to build a legacy for myself and for her long-term. I wanted to be able to show her the example of what being a business owner, being an entrepreneur, being a real estate investor can provide for you and show her along the way what it takes to buy and sell real estate. It's something that she's learning right now. She goes with me on property tours. She attends a lot of investor workshops with me. She may not understand the details yet, but she's learning that Dad buys and sells real estate. Dad gets to snowboard or go boating whenever we want. There's very few limitations for us now that we've built a successful real estate business. She'll be growing up in this environment, surrounded by real estate investors. I think she'll have a completely different legacy and outlook because of the upbringing that I'll be putting her in as far as being entrepreneur and real estate investor.

She'll be much more advanced as far as financial literacy goes because of what I'll be able to teach her. I think that'll be hugely beneficial. My legacy is passing it on to the next generation.

In addition to that, I teach and train real estate investors on a weekly basis, and I love doing that. I have as much fun, if not more fun, working with new, novice investors than I do with my investor partners and my capital partners. It's fun to make a lot of money, but it's also just as much fun to teach and train people who I see are in their early 20s and starting out and thinking back to the time when I was starting and thinking about who was it that helped me along the way and how can I help other people along the way. That helps me out. It helps me become a better investor myself because being able to teach and train people that I know helps me solidify the stuff that I'd already learned, and then they can go out and find us real estate deals. They can get paid on them. I'm helping people make money for themselves. That brings a lot of satisfaction to me when I see other people making money from the creative strategies that we're helping them do. And finally, Cole Hatter, who got me started investing in real estate has taught me the value of Making Money Matter, giving away money to charity and finding a higher purpose than making money just for ourselves; its important to give back, so I have several at-risk youth organizations that I'm involved in now and I can contribute my time and donations towards. Being able to make a difference in today's youth through entrepreneurship and education is where I'd like to leave a legacy.

Roxanne Young & Keith Miyamoto

Roxanne Young was born and raised in Hawaii. She came from a very close knit family, and with five other brothers and sisters, there was always something to learn, someone to live up to, and something to share. She graduated from Seattle University with a double major in Educational/Criminal Psychology and Foreign Language and Literature. She has studied at the Gymnasium in Karlsruhe, Germany, and the University of Graz, in Graz, Austria. She has always had a love of foreign languages and has continued to study multiple languages over the years. That, paired with her love for travel, has taken her around the world studying and working in Asia, Europe, Costa Rica, and throughout the United States and Canada.

Described as an adventurer by her friends and family, she has learned how to get paid to travel, write off just about all of her trips, and expand her businesses throughout the world. She decided, if she was going to continue traveling, she should learn something that would be global, so she went back to school and got an MBA in Global Management. Working in Human Resources and helping to complete a corporate merger, that left 1500 of her co-workers unemployed, she decided that corporate America was just not for her. And after seeing what her parents went through towards the end of their careers, she decided that she would never let anyone determine her paycheck ever again.

Roxanne's work history would most certainly qualify her as "a jack of all trades." She has worked in every industry one could imagine. Her strength is that of a master networker—she has been able to connect people to others who have benefited from the new relationship. A thirst for knowledge and a hearty work ethic has resulted in six businesses that allow her the benefits of freedom! When asked about her life's purpose, she is very clear in knowing that "God's purpose for her is to help inspire others and offer hope; to live as good a life as possible so others know that they can do the same." Live by doing because people do what you do, not by what you say.

Born and raised in sports and outdoor activities, she still starts just about every day out in the ocean, surfing with a few hundred of her best friends. Every day, she has to pinch herself as the sun rises as she appreciates the fact that she lives in such a beautiful place and is so fortunate to be able to enjoy it as well. Most people in Hawaii have multiple jobs and have really had to sacrifice time with their family and their health in order to make ends meet. Roxanne just wants to be able to take care of all of her family and have time with them on her terms.

Keith Miyamoto, her husband, grew up in a true blue-collar town in Pennsylvania and was barely making a living paycheck to paycheck like everyone else he knew. Coming from a very conservative upbringing, he was taught the mindset that he had to go to school, get a good job, and just do what you're told. Until meeting Roxanne, he probably would not have ever thought of owning his own business, though he possessed all the skills and training to do so.

Keith graduated from Rider College with a double B.S. in Computer Science and Accounting. Since then he has amassed a wealth of business knowledge by working in various industries such as hospitality, retail, government, banking, insurance, manufacturing, and retirement. He is currently working as a manager within the information technology field and has to put in long hours and is on call 24/7. He realizes that he is a slave to his job and that there is more to life.

When the two met, he was actually attending real estate school and was looking to spend his weekends as a real estate agent. After getting some additional education, the two realized that with a full-time job that took most of his energy 12-hours a day, that extra time could be spent on building an investment portfolio which would be a much better investment of his time.

Working in the retirement industry, he has realized that most people are not able to fully retire on their retirement benefits. This has led him to realize that passive or residual income is a means to financial freedom and a happy retirement.

Their dream is to inspire others to live their dreams and to make this world a better place. As part of that, they hope to adopt children and provide them with a loving home and the skills that will help them to think outside the box. They are working to be able to have the financial resources and time to spend it with them.

Shannon:
What inspired you to get into real estate investing?

Roxanne:
My mother and father were both real estate agents at one time or another, that along with their corporate jobs; they did whatever they had to do, to take care of the six of us. They are truly amazing people! They have instilled in us, the most amazing work ethic. So many people talk about passing things onto their children, but the reality is, when you can pass integrity, compassion, tenacity, and work ethic onto your kids, there isn't anything your kids won't be able to handle, that is the true legacy you leave.

My mom always told me, "you should get into real estate." It was not something that I really couldn't see myself doing—lived that life, my whole life, was not interested. Our family has a lot of investment property that we've worked on throughout my childhood. Both my parents have real estate investments today and are living comfortable lives and have been able to leave a legacy for their children and even their grand-children.

So what changed for me after all these years? Well, when I was living in Seattle, I attended a "Nothing Down" seminar, which kind of got me interested again in the thought of "owning" property. It was enough to get me interested in buying something as an investment. I was mentored by some fairly well-known RE Gurus and a few dynamic mentors. So that lit the fire...

Shannon:

What changed for you?

Roxanne:

So, as I shared, I attended a RE Guru event, spent the weekend learning "all" that I needed to know to purchase a property for "nothing down" and own my first rental, or so I thought. However, the most important thing that I learned from that whole experience is that I learned just enough to be dangerous. I made an offer on a property, got the property, did the fix, rented it out, and I thought I was doing well, it was stressful, challenging and still kind of exciting.

For the first year it was pretty good. The third year, apparently, I rented to a bad tenant, it was a BIG mistake. That ended up in turning my cute little house into a drug house with shot gun holes in my basement and needles everywhere. I off loaded it for no profit and a lot of headache, but it was a great learning experience still. Following that experience, I was not all that excited to get back into the RE market. I have always had friends who did well in real estate over the years but never thought we would have the skills and knowledge to make this our business.

I recently got married and through various educational endeavors, business ventures, and life situations, my husband and I realized that in order for us to retire before we were 80 and live our lives the way we wanted to, we had to do something different than what we've been doing. And needless to say, I have to finally admit that "mom was right!' LOL! Real estate was the best way to create long-term wealth. Through our education, we learned how to flip both mortgages and how to be our own bank and things just grew from there! We now own four properties both in Hawaii and in the mainland. We learned how to use OPM (Other People's Money) to create capital to fund our businesses and our real estate deals. Today we have six businesses, our real estate investments, and my husband is almost out of his FT job.

Out of all of these businesses, I have to say the ones that I cherish are those that produce passive or residual income. In addition, we get to enjoy the tax write offs which save us thousands of dollars on our taxable income and are able to travel extensively every year. Why anyone would still want to still work a FT job is beyond my comprehension.

My husband always tells people that before he met me, his world was so small, he didn't know what he was missing out on. Now we travel at least five times a year together and have a large circle of friends that inspire us to be better and who help us navigate life at a whole other level. Now we have a passion for helping others because we've been in the darkness and sometimes, you just don't know that you're there until you see someone else's light.

I think that if I had some help navigating my way through the process, it would have been a completely different experience. So you live and learn. Hopefully I'm a lot smarter now. I have a little bit more education and I have better resources, which is phenomenal. And that has made all the difference.

Shannon:
If someone was going to start in real estate investing, what would you recommend they do first?

Roxanne:
Honestly, if you don't know anything about real estate or just investments as a whole, I would start by playing the game of cash flow with people who know and do real estate investment. Our group does High Velocity cash flow where we use all the strategies we have learned and apply it to deals in the game; it's bringing in real life application at no risk. This has probably singlehandedly been the most beneficial activity that we've done to apply the tools that we have learned. Education is important but investing in RE is scary, so being able to

apply what you've learned is invaluable because with practice comes confidence, with confidence comes action, with action you can create deals, and through deals comes wealth.

Better to make mistakes with zero risk than to do it in real life and lose your shirt. Why would you want to play a game? You learn what your relationship to money is and how you tend to use it. The next step is to get the education necessary to do this business, learn from people who are actively doing investments, not just teaching it. Mistakes are costly in real estate and business in general.

The way you reduce "risk" in business is to have applicable knowledge and surround yourself with a team that compliments your talents. Having a community that learns from one another, that is willing to share resources, information, and talents is vital to a less stressful experience in real estate. Pooling your resources with people you know and trust is invaluable in this business.

Shannon:
I bet it is. So how has your education in real estate changed the way that you invest?

Roxanne:
Having the education that is accessible at my best study times and anywhere I go is vital to my ability to fit it into my schedule and lifestyle. Having access to resources like listings, applications, and IOS systems that help us do what we do better, faster, and smarter is priceless. While most people are pounding the pavement to look for property and deals, we have a short cut that plugs us into all the most current resources that looks for the properties for us. We just set up our parameters and ask it to bring us deals.

I used to look at Craigslist, read the paper, and scour the For-Sale ads till the cows came home. I can't even remember the last time I did that now that we have this new IOS system. It's super exciting!

Our education also plugs us into Real Deal Tours and Deal or No Deal meetings where we can run our deals by our community to brainstorm offers, renovation strategies, exit strategies, etc. It's kind of an amazing group to be a part of. Who does that these days?

I like the fact that we have documents at our disposal. Everyone knows that there is so much paperwork associated with real estate transactions, so much to know and so much to do, dotting your "I"s and crossing your "T"s. This has been so helpful.

How has it changed the way I invest? Well, it has provided me with options to finance, to purchase, to sell, and to negotiate the deals. One size does not fit all, but with the proper education, well, the world is your oyster—there is no "ONE" way to do a deal, it all depends on what the client needs out of the deal. We learn that we are problem solvers and we look to help others using our knowledge and ability to apply that knowledge.

Shannon:
The question is, how do you minimize the risks of investing so that you can maximize success?

Roxanne:
Minimize risk by getting educated. Maximize benefit by practicing your trade. Do the actions that get you results and get good at doing this business, then you'll be better at applying the tools to your business. Pick a specific strategy, get as good at it as you can, do it over and over again, apply it, then run your deal by someone you trust who has experience. Learn the process of initiating the deal and what questions need to be answered before it's a done deal.

Shannon:
How have mentors in your real estate investing helped you navigate potential pit falls?

Roxanne:
Having good mentors can make all the difference in the world. You can take the hard way, or you can take the right way. I've always had wonderful mentors in my life: mentors for health, money, business, and life. We must surround ourselves with people who inspire us to be better than we ever thought possible. Find mentors who inspire you, challenge you, who tell you what you need to hear, not what you

want to hear. They should help you to discover answers on your own so you can develop skills to think your way through any type of situation. Sometimes Mentors help you to walk through a deal before you actually pull the trigger to ensure that you're covering the important details. Learning how your mentors think, process, and act are skills that you can transfer to the rest of your life. Find a mentor who walks his/her talk. We learn by watching, not necessarily by what someone tells us. I remember those days as a kid, my parents used to say, 'do what I say, not what I do.'... Well, kids will always do what you do not what you say. That keeps them accountable to us and us to them.

Shannon:
What is cash flow and why should it be such an important focus of your business?

Roxanne:
Oh my gosh. So cash flow basically is your income and then you minus off all of your monthly expenses (CF = Income – Expense). It's whatever is left over at the end of the month after you pay all your bills. Cash flow really is the amount of spending power or investment power that you have once all your bills have been paid. And of course, the larger your cash flow, the more possibilities you have.

Most people don't realize they have cash flow because any leftover money at the end of the month is usually spent on "stuff" or liabilities that add no value to your life. Learning how to use your cash flow to create more cash flow really is the key to long-term freedom. We like to teach others to have their cash flow working for them.

I think playing a game like cash flow teaches you: 1) what kind of relationship you have with money, 2) what your hang-ups are with money, 3) what your risk thresholds are when using money, and 4) the benefits of working with a team rather than just working by yourself. If you can learn to use the cash flow for investments, then turn around and use the proceeds for your doodads, you now have used your cash flow to fund your dreams! It's such a beautiful thing! You have choices in life. You can either work hard for your money or you can have your money work hard for you.

Shannon:

If you're starting with little money or poor credit, what are some strategies that you can use to get into real estate investing?

Roxanne:

My favorite way to fund any project is using OPM (Other People's Money). Why would you want to use your own money when you could use OPM? If you have poor credit, there are things you can do to improve your credit quickly; in the meantime, you may have to look for alternate resources to help fund your projects. We all come to the table with different kinds of currency: financial currency (money), intellectual currency (knowledge), relationship currency (our network), time currency (time) and skill currency (talents). Learn what you can bring to the table and seek out others who can bring the rest.

You have to be teachable and learn skills to increase your financial Intelligence. Many people think that the lack of money means that you can't do any of this. Yes, you need money to invest, but no one says it has to be YOUR money. Seek out people who are rich where you are not. Create a team of people who have the currency that you do not yet possess, and you have the makings of a winning team. If you're in a canoe and you're not paddling the canoe, you're dead weight and might be tossed overboard. Be someone of value to the team; bring your best, be your best, and ADD to the team dynamics.

If you can do this, there are no limits to what you and your team can accomplish. It's truly priceless!

Shannon:

I bet it is. What is one of the top real estate strategies you have learned?

Roxanne:

My favorite real estate strategy that I've learned is creative financing. I love looking at deals and then trying to figure out ways to NOT use our own money to fund the deal. Use OPM to fund deals, and help the funder make money that they normally wouldn't be making if they kept their money in a bank. I also LOVE all the ways that you can save money doing this kind of business. Tax and legal strategies help you keep more of your money, like hiring your kids to decrease your income tax and saving tons of money by reducing your interest expense. It's really exciting to be a part of changing the lives of other and giving then hope for a brighter future.

Shannon:

Is real estate investing success dependent on a strong economy?

Roxanne:

I recall a good friend who worked as a fire fighter; he said, "When there is RED (fire), they make GREEN (money)." Because, you know, opportunity is everywhere. There is money to be made in any kind of economy. It's all how you look at things. Some people see only obstacles and reason why they can't; still others see opportunity around every corner. As an investor, the best time to buy property is when you can find a great deal to help people solve their problems. The trick is to be prepared if something comes available. Someone with an investor mindset constantly seeks opportunity in a problem looking to be solved.

I was once told that history always repeats itself—the better armed you are when the tides turn, the more resilient you'll be to come out of it. You MUST dig your well before you're thirsty. The problem is that most people wait until the drought before even thinking about digging their well. By then, it's too late. We hope to change that, one person at a time. If we can teach parents what we do, we hope that they will teach their children by example, and if we can do that, we will raise all of society. Imagine having a community of individuals with increased financial literacy, skills to help them navigate the industry, and more resilience to change. Wouldn't that be a wonderful world to live in?

Shannon:

When doing a fix and flip, what do you want to look out for?

Roxanne:

Well, we look for a good area that has profit potential. Better to buy the worst house in the best neighborhood. I like purposeful neighborhoods;

if we're looking for single family dwellings, I check the school district, crime rate, sales over the last six months, and developments that are in the plans. I look at what the median price is for the houses that are similar, the comps. I look for basically what the history of the house has been. How long has it been on the market? Has it been listed multiple times? Are there any special circumstances that need to be addressed like foundation and roofing? The cost of fixing the house, of course, and the amount of profitability you think you can get out of doing the deal. And a nice price would be good too. Ideally, we look for below market value; however, still being able to help out the people who are selling it. There is an endless list of what to look for, so do your homework and make sure to cover as many as possible. I guess the bottom line is the actual potential of success for everyone.

Shannon:

If someone wanted to invest in multi-family dwellings, what do they need to know?

Roxanne:

Oh, that's my favorite. I haven't done it yet, but my dream is to own a building and have my office in one of the units and then rent out the rest. I think for multi-family units, I like duplexes and four-plexes. I think those are really nice. Possibly an eight or ten-plex would probably be my max. You definitely have to know about any lease issues.

I'm not sure how it is in the rest of the country, but Hawaii has this thing called "lease-hold" which is where someone can buy the unit but they don't own the property. Fee simple means that you own the land and your dwelling. We also have co-ops here where everyone gets a say in who moves in and out of the building. These are all "need to know" aspects of owning a multi-family dwelling. For investors, however, these buildings can create good opportunities depending on the length left on the lease. Our dream is to have duplexes and four-plexes all over the country and using them to put our children up through school, teaching them to run a business, and writing off their school expenses. Imagine having your children leave school understanding mortgages, understanding cash flow, and knowing how to create investments instead of debt. There is so much awesomeness in that vision!

Shannon:

So, if you were looking at a property and it was a leasehold property, would that always eliminate you from purchasing?

Roxanne:

No, I think it depends on how long you have the lease and what the possibilities are in the future for renegotiating that lease or possibly purchasing the lease. In Hawaii, you can pick up these deals super cheap, a $260k property that is towards the end of a 50-year lease, let's say 10-20 years left, you could pick this up pretty cheap, maybe $30-60k. You could either rent it out and make some money, or you could live in it for a great price.

Shannon:

What is the number one mistake an individual makes when buying their first investment property?

Roxanne:

The number one mistake is probably being too quick to do the deal and not doing your due diligence before buying. Sometimes the excitement of the deal blinds us to what still needs to be done. Also, not giving themselves an exit strategy; I mean, even putting in an offer, there are certain things that you need to put in an offer in case something happens and you decide you don't want the property— you have to be able to get out of it someway.

Shannon:

Do you have a favorite exit strategy?

Roxanne:

My favorite exit strategy is the one I use to save me from a bad deal or that makes me the best profit out of the current deal that I'm in. I know that's a little vague, but the reality is that they are all good and all have their time and place. I love being able to exit a property by selling it to the tenant and being the bank. Lease options are something I love because it allows us to help families get into a home, rather than rent. And I don't have to be a landlord which has always been my goal. And it's a WIN/WIN for everyone! They get a home and I get a monthly check which supplements my monthly cash flow! Whoo Hoo!

Shannon:

Perfect. What advice would you give to someone who is allowing fear to hold them back from starting their real estate investing?

Roxanne:

"Live in faith, not in fear... There is no such thing as fear. Fear is only the absence of faith."

Having faith in what you know, in the person you are, in the people around you and in the things you spend your time on will carry you through any difficulties. Fear and faith cannot exist simultaneously; you have to choose one over the other. If you're afraid, start with the cash flow game, practice what you learn, and implement it in the game and slowly in real life. Surround yourself with people who can help you grow personally and professionally.

Shannon:

When you began your real estate investing career, how important was it to establish a team to help you be successful?

Roxanne:

Your community is so vital because you can't possibly be good at all things; focused individuals are more skilled than most Jack of all Trades. So creating a team of specialists makes for a well-balanced team. The way our education works, it creates a team of experts from which you can draw experience all in one place. Creating a good team can really open up so many more avenues and possibilities for you. Rather than just doing it by yourself.

Shannon:

What is a tax lien?

Roxanne:

I fell in love with the concepts of tax liens and tax deeds. When I learned about being able to acquire property for pennies on the dollar, I just flipped out.

Liens are put on properties when taxes are not paid, some come from the counties, states, or even the federal government. County tax liens are the oldest liens around because they go as far back as the establishment of the United States. The monies are used to fund the community: roads, schools, maintenance, etc. When people fail to pay their taxes, the agency can attach a lien to the property and that property cannot be sold until those liens are paid off. If the owner does not pay the liens before the redemption period, the county can sell the house… there is a lot more to it than that, but you get the gist.

Shannon:

What happens if they don't pay their taxes?

Roxanne:

If they don't pay their taxes, they still have a redemption period in which they can still payoff the taxes. The counties give them as much time as they possibly can to get current with their taxes. During this time, they still need money to fund schools, roads, etc. so what they do is sell the tax lien to investors; they get their money and in return for that, the investor gets a good rate of return, more than what they would get at a bank. It's a little involved and complicated, but you would have the opportunity to be able to foreclose on the property, if you're in the correct position.

Shannon:

What about if they do end up paying those taxes? So now you can't fore-close on the property. So do you lose your money?

Roxanne:

No, if it is paid off, the tax lien holder will get the initial investment back plus the fee charged by the county. It's a great investment. Where else can you get 18 percent to 24 percent return on your investment? Certainly not the bank!

Shannon:

That's not bad at all. Thank you. In your business, how do you help other people learn more about real estate?

Roxanne:

I just love to share what I've learned, what I've been able to do, things that my friends have done. What I've learned is that there are so many people out there who are "unconscious incompetents": they don't know that they don't know. Imagine if you can shed a little light on that and suddenly, they are hungry to learn more, and that starts them on the path of "I can do it too!" Most people just don't know that there are other ways. You never know, you could be the answer to the prayers they have been praying for years. How amazing would that be to be able to free others from their financial imprisonment. There is education available to learn alternatives and people around who can help you implement them to produce change. And to be part of their growth process, it is unbelievable. Who does that these days?

Shannon:

What are some creative ways to acquire a property?

Roxanne:

What if there was a way to know when properties were about to go to market? Or a way to know, before everyone else knows, that people are about to be foreclosed on and are looking for a solution? Or if there was a way to help people figure out creative financing and help them keep their property? Be a good friend and listen to people's problems. What if your house was falling apart and you didn't have the financial resources to fix it up yourself, but you wouldn't be able to sell it unless you fixed it up? What if all these situations were looking for solutions? Would that be a great way to acquire property?

Shannon:

You know, most millionaires and billionaires have investments in commercial real estate. Why do you think that is?

Roxanne:

One of my best friends owns a ton of commercial property in this state. And he is phenomenal. He's probably one of my best mentors. I think for a commercial property, when you lease space, oftentimes, you not only get your lease rent, you also get a percentage of their revenue. That income is the ultimate passive income because the better they do, the better you do. I love passive income!

Shannon:

What is that?

Roxanne:

Passive income is when you do the work once and get paid over and over again. Nearly all the population, 97 percent, trade hours for dollars, doctors, lawyers, bakers, etc. Just because they have a title doesn't mean that they are excluded from that group. What most people don't understand is that people who earn passive income have done a lot of work and received no pay for a long time. They invest in themselves and in the end when those checks start coming in, they finally getting paid. What most people don't understand about passive income is that it's not "get rich quick money;" you always still have to do the work and most times you work harder and don't get paid.

I look at passive income as the "Great Harvest" income. You plant seeds (develop your idea), you cultivate the crop (do the actions that create the behaviors), you feed it (through consistency), and you harvest once all of the work has been done and cash in at the market when it's sold. Real estate is no different; you still have to sift through a bunch of deals, make a bunch of offers, and sometimes you think its sprouting, then the next thing you know, it's dead. Look at the Chinese Bamboo plant, it takes years to grow a small sprout, about five years, but come year six and the bamboo will grow tall and strong and will live a resilient life. I remember my mom, when she first got into real estate, I couldn't understand how she could go so many years without making a sale and spend all that time on it. But she stuck it out, and her first deal was a million-dollar property. She made more from that deal than a year's wages at her FT job. Now that's perseverance.

Shannon:

So, if passive income is so great, why don't we all have passive income?

Roxanne:

Most people are taught to trade hours for dollars. If you've ever learned about the Cash Flow Quadrant by Robert Kiyosaki, he talks about how we move from employee, to sole-proprietor business, to a business where others are working for you, then to Investments that bring in money without you even being there. Our society is so focused on instant gratification. Anything worthwhile is an uphill journey, but most of us are stuck in downhill habits. (John Maxwell's famous words)

When you work for yourself, if you don't show up, you don't get paid. I think the single greatest difference between the wealthy and the status quo is that the wealthy know they can create wealth. The poor find reasons why they do not have wealth. I've been an entrepreneur since I was 13-years old, probably even earlier than that. I've never worried about money, not because I had it, but because I always know that I can make it. Drop me in any city, in any country, and I can create a job or business.

Perhaps that's it. People will bet on the tables in Las Vegas, but ask them to bet on themselves? I think few will take that bet. I love entrepreneurs; they just think differently. They are educated risk takers, even when they are conservative. They have faith in the process which instills faith in their ideas, which spills over to faith in themselves.

There are many kinds of passive incomes: there's real estate, direct sales, music, books, art, ideas, apps—the list is endless. I guess I would like to challenge everyone to Increase their cash flow by implementing just ONE passive income idea which can help to create some great supplementary income for you, making money while you sleep. If you have a hang up about it, think of it this way... you support "passive income for someone else every day." If you pay rent, if you re-order anything more than once, you're participating in passive income. You're supplying passive income to someone else. The main reason why most people won't entertain the idea of passive income is truly because of ignorance. The good news is that ignorance is not permanent and is easily remedied. Get educated before saying "NO" to anything in this life. You might be missing the greatest opportunity of your life. Go passive!

Woody Woodward

Woody Woodward dropped out of high school at age 16, was a millionaire by 26 and flat broke by age 27. After clawing his way out of financial ruin he built four different multi-million dollar companies before he turned 40. Through overcoming this adversity Mr. Woodward has become a best-selling author of fifteen books about turning tragedy into triumph. Having interviewed over 2,500 people around the world for his research, he is the pioneer and founder of *Your Emotional Fingerprint*™. Understanding this cutting edge human technology allows one to strip back the layers of excuses and build a proper foundation for mass achievement in one's personal life, relationships and career. Emotional Fingerprint was chosen as one of the leading techniques to be presented to the United Nations to assist them in reaching their millennial goals.

His latest project is inspiring entrepreneurs with M.O.N.E.Y. Matrix™ daily videos that help them reach their goals, make more money and find fulfillment in their careers. He has shared his cutting edge techniques on ABC, CBS, NBC, FOX and Forbes.

Contact Info:
www.GetMoneyMatrix.com
www.MeetWoody.com

Shannon:

According to Forbes Magazine, real estate is one of the top three ways that people become wealthy. As a real estate expert, why do you feel that this is the case?

Woody:

Real estate is the only investment I know of where you have a tangible, physical product that, even if the market goes down, you can still use. Yes, you can say stocks are tangible, but in reality they're not. Yes, you can lease them out, you can do calls and you can do puts on them, but with real estate, even if the market crashes, you can physically rent that property. You get a tax write-off if you are renting the property; so to me, real estate has always been, looking back in history, one of the top ways to generate revenue.

Shannon:

Do you have an opinion on whether commercial real estate or residential real estate is a better investment?

Woody:

I have friends who do both. I personally have always done residential. As for my friends who do commercial real estate it adds a zero to their net worth. If you're going to make a hundred thousand dollars on flipping a residential property, you'll make about a million flipping a commercial property; so it's the same game, just bigger numbers. If you have the resources to do it, most billionaires do it in commercial property, not residential. A lot of millionaires do residential property.

Shannon:

How hard is it to get started in residential real estate if you don't have a lot of money?

Woody:

That's the great thing about residential versus commercial; it doesn't take hardly anything with residential. Nowadays, you can still put down 3 percent or 5 percent on a home to buy it and then flip it, or to let it appreciate and sell it in the future and make additional revenue by leasing it, or there are a lot of different techniques where you can do owner financing. Owner financing is when the seller can't sell a home, maybe it's a bad market, and they're willing to carry that note for you; so in essence, the seller becomes the bank and you're buying it directly from the seller. You then still have all the legal rights to that property, so you can rent it out, you can fix it up, you can sell it; you can do whatever you want, as long as the seller's paid in full when you sell that home.

Shannon:

When the seller's paid in full, how does that benefit them if they're the bank? How do they buy another house?

Woody:

There is only one of two reasons why a seller will finance, in my experience. First is that they have enough income on their own, but they're happy just to sell it because they want to get a higher interest rate. Right now, if you put your money in the bank, you're going to get maybe 1 or 1.5 percent. If they carry the note on that home for you, they can charge you 5, 7, even 10 percent, so they're making more money on their own money, so they become a bank.

The other reason is that sometimes in a bad market they just can't sell a home. Let's say they owe $200,000 on a home and the home's only worth $175,000, so they physically can't sell it unless they come up with the $25,000 difference; so they'll carry their loan for you, and then as the market changes and goes back up and the home's worth $250,000, you can then sell it and keep that extra $50,000 since you bought it for $200,000. Then they are happy because now they get their $200,000 out that they already owe their bank, and it becomes a little win-win.

Shannon:

When you're actually looking for homes in a down market situation where people are upside down in their homes, do you look at the location? Do you look at the future projections for businesses, neighborhoods, etc.?

Woody:

Absolutely. The number one thing that you hear people always talk about with real estate, the number one technique, is location, location, location. I've had friends who have literally bought corner lots and then they heard that Walmart was coming across the street. This happened to a friend of mind in California who bought the lot for $150,000 and had the owner carry the note. Six months later Walmart announced that they were building across the street. His lot went from $150,000 to $500,000 literally overnight. He would be able to sell that and take that money. Now he can play in the commercial business on a little bit larger level.

Most investor works the same way. You make a little bit, you turn that money over. It's really called compounding interest where you take your principle and your interest and then you roll it over again into the next property. There's also a great tax benefit to that as well. You don't have to pay tax on that money as long as you're rolling it over in to a property of equal or higher value.

Shannon:

What do you think is the number one mistake that an individual makes when buying their first investment property?

Woody:

The number one reason why people make mistakes on their first investment property is they don't have a mentor. They don't have someone to follow. They don't have someone that can show them the right thing to do. They just hear their buddies doing it, they go out and they buy a home, but they haven't done all the certification, they haven't verified that this property's not going to have termite issues or meth issues, or something else that could really hurt them. They think, "Oh, it's a good deal, I can buy that and make a ton of money." The benefit to real estate is there's tons of people and there's tons of organizations out there that have already done it a thousand times, so connect with them. Join an investment club, join a company that does education, and then they'll help you limit your potential risk.

Shannon:

How have your mentors in real estate investing helped you to navigate pitfalls?

Woody:

We don't know what we don't know, and every deal has a potential problem, and every deal tends to really have a problem. I'm in the middle of a transaction right now where the home had to be lifted. We knew that there were some cracks in the foundation, but we weren't sure; so before we actually took ownership and before we actually even wrote the contract, we had an engineer come out. The only reason I did that is my mentor recommended, "You know what Woody, if you've got cracks in your foundation that are larger than average, hire an engineer. Spend the six, seven, eight hundred dollars. You'll save hundreds of thousands of dollars of potential losses for a small investment", so we did that and it ended up costing the seller $75,000 to raise that foundation. Had we bought that home not knowing that, we'd be out $75,000, so an $800 investment saved me $75,000.

Now, after the home was raised, we paid another $400 for an inspector to go out and verify absolutely everything. What he did is he pulled off all of the insulation in the basement and found another crack that we didn't know about, so now we're having another company come out and verify that crack because you can see daylight through the foundation. That's never good. You never want to see daylight in the foundation.

They're coming out to fix that. Once again, the seller will have to pay that and we won't.

Shannon:

How do you help other people learn more about real estate?

Woody:

Everybody has that friend who is in real estate. I'm that friend for my friends, and they will always ask me, "Woody what about this?" Or, "What about that transaction? What about that home you flipped?" What I like to do is just invite them to come along and take a look.

There's times where I'll take five of my friends and show them a house that I'm doing, show them the pitfalls and mistakes, and where's the benefit to changing it.

This one home, there is about $100,000 in equity from us just buying it right. I believe that when it comes to real estate, you make your money when you buy it, not when you sell it, so you have to buy it right.

Shannon:

You are obviously passionate about real estate. What actually inspired you to get into the industry?

Woody:

I grew up with my folks in a different generation where my dad was the traditional father who would always work and my mother would stay home. In the 80's when the market crashed and we didn't have a lot of money, it was a challenge, and so my mom became a realtor. She would list homes, so when I was very young, I'd go with my mom when she would go list a home. I'd walk through these homes and they were, to a kid, like a jungle gym. They were just so fascinating, and I grew up being exposed to real estate. I met some of the investors who my mom was selling for and it changed my life forever.

If you list a home as a typical realtor, you'll make 3 percent. The investor can make 10 to 20 percent. They're just taking the greater risk. The realtor doesn't have any risk. They have some advertising costs, but that's not a huge risk. The investor who bought the home, fixed it up, put new paint/carpet in, now is making $50,000, $100,000, $150,000 on a transaction. That blew my mind, and that was the second I knew I wanted to be in real estate.

Shannon:

What are some of the creative ways that you use now, or what is your favorite way to find a property to acquire a fix and flip?

Woody:

For me the best way to find property is to know your area, so back to location, location, location. The home that I'm buying right now, the one that had the sunken basement, we've been trying for two years to get this home. We've talked to the seller, he wouldn't sell it to us. Then low and behold we found out that he passed away, and then we went to his heirs, which was his older sister. Well, she's eighty-four years old. She doesn't want to deal with this property. She lives out of state, but because I was driving around, just driving by this one house that I've always wanted to acquire, I saw a car there. I knew he lived out of state. It was an investment property for him, so when I saw a car there, I just knocked on the door. And told them that because the home had been vacant for over three years, that's why it was neglected and the home sunk. Basically, I was able to get the home before it even went on the market.

Had they taken the time to invest in the property, to fix it up, and then to sell it, I would've been out of the loop. So to me the best technique is, take an area, a geographical area that you know well and trust, and then master it. Know every house. You can pull titles. You can find out when people are delinquent. You can ask them to buy the home before it goes into foreclosure. There are so many techniques to save yourself time because it's trying to find that jewel in the rough. It's always hard to find, but when you find one, you can pull out fifty to a hundred grand.

Shannon:
How do you decide if you are going to fix and flip a home or buy and hold it for rental income?

Woody:
If I'm in a financial position where I can hold it and I can keep it long-term and I believe a certain area geographically is going to go up in value, then I will hold it. I have done holds in the past, but on the fix and flips, those are the ones that give you large pops. Wealthy people, I believe, get wealthy by the large pops–fifty grand, a hundred grand, two hundred and fifty grand pops. I've made $200,000 on a house in thirty days. I can't save that much money myself, I can't save my way to wealth, and I don't believe most people can. You look at CEOs who have large stock options and a buyout takes place; they

get a large pop of millions of dollars, so to create massive wealth, you've got to have large pops.

Well, as soon as you've had enough large pops where you've got a good nest egg, now you can afford to buy one, hold it, and if a renter does not pay, you can afford to make that monthly payment. I don't believe in being house poor. If you own a bunch of properties but you can't fix up the yard or you can't take a vacation, I call that being house poor. You may have a million dollars in real estate, but you can't afford to take a vacation, then you don't have the life that real estate's designed to give you.

Shannon:
I'd like to go back to when you said you saw the car and you just knocked on the door. Tell me how that conversation went?

Woody:
It's very simple. You can tell when somebody is stressed. You can see it on their face. This woman looked bewildered. This is the first time she had seen this home after her brother passed. She didn't want that property. She lives two thousand miles away. She wants nothing to do with this property. I asked her, "You know what, I've been watching this home for two years. Are you the new owner? She said, "Yeah, my brother passed, and now I have inherited this home." I said, "Well, what is your intention? Do you want to sell the home, or do you want to keep it and rent it out? What would you like to do?" "Oh my gosh, I just want to sell this home," she replied, so I gave her an offer on the spot. She turned it down. I waited about a month. I kept checking on the home. I saw them doing yard work trying to fix it up. I went back to her, I said, "You know what, are you by chance interested in selling the home yet?" At that point, she was, because she just realized how much work it was going to be to fix it up.

You have to understand that if someone is going to sell you a house at a discount than what it should be going for, that means there's inherently something wrong with the home. Either it needs new carpet, or they had pets in there, or it smells. It's been neglected. Things are broken. So when you're looking for a fix and flip, they're never in perfect condition, otherwise they'd get top of the retail value. People who have these homes don't want them because they know how much it's going to cost to fix it, and that was the case with her, so it was really easy to buy it from her, to take that pressure and stress off of her.

Shannon:

Do you think that you can have real estate success being a one- man-show, or do you think that most people need to have a team?

Woody:

When I say I'm a one-man show I don't want to imply that I don't have a team and I don't work with other people because that's not true. I don't have employees that I pay that help me run my company, but I have a network of people that I work with. In real estate you cannot be successful without a network of people. It's impossible. You need to know a title guy, a realtor. You need to know an appraiser. There are so many moving parts in real estate, you need to have a group of people you work with.

When it comes to education, I go back to that saying, "We don't know what we don't know." Create an environment and a network, facilitate a mastermind, put people who are in real estate in the same room and you will expedite your knowledge. You'll expedite your learning curves. It is crucial that you spend time with a team of people who have your best interest in mind to make you successful.

Shannon:

What is your favorite investment strategy when the market is good and homes are selling quickly?

Woody:

In California in 2005 when the market was just exploding and homes were appreciating at 30 percent a year, if you bought a home for $400,000, in a year it was going for a $520,000, so in that market we were buying homes that weren't even built yet. When a new subdivision was under construction we would put down $5,000. Homes would take six months to nine months to build. By the time we bought that home and moved into it, we already had $60,000 to $80,000 of appreciation; so in an up market my favorite thing to do is speculation. Know an area, know where the parks and schools are being built, buy homes that are under construction so that you can flip them as soon as you close on them.

Shannon:

When you look at everything that you do in your life, your real estate investing career, your entrepreneurial adventures, and your life married with children, what legacy do you want to leave?

Woody:

I want my children and the people that I have the opportunity to come in contact with to realize that they can change. Regardless of your past, regardless of where you started, you can change. I believe real estate is one of the greatest agents for change. It allows someone, even an uneducated person like myself, to learn something, to master something, and then to make a very good income with it.

My legacy is that I want people to realize they can do it. That's the bottom line, that they can have their own life, that they can change, that they can become who they want to become regardless of their background.

As my wife would say, "We are just borrowing it for a time before the next generation borrows it." Since we don't take anything with us, I would want my legacy to be the impact I have had on my relationships. There is no doubt my life has been better because of the lives of others. I would like to do the same for someone else.